Forms of Validity in Research

David Brinberg, Louise H. Kidder, *Editors*

NEW DIRECTIONS FOR METHODOLOGY OF SOCIAL AND BEHAVIORAL SCIENCE
DONALD W. FISKE, *Editor-in-Chief*

Number 12, June 1982

Paperback sourcebooks in
The Jossey-Bass Social and Behavioral Sciences Series

Jossey-Bass Inc., Publishers
San Francisco • Washington • London

Forms of Validity in Research
Number 12, June 1982
      David Brinberg, Louise H. Kidder, *Editors*

New Directions for Methodology of Social and Behavioral Science Series
Donald W. Fiske, *Editor-in-Chief*

New Directions for Methodology of Social and Behavioral Science
is published quarterly by Jossey-Bass Inc., Publishers.
Subscriptions, single-issue orders, change of address notices,
undelivered copies, and other correspondence should be sent to
New Directions Subscriptions, Jossey-Bass Inc., Publishers,
433 California Street, San Francisco, California 94104.

Editorial correspondence should be sent to the Editor-in-Chief,
Donald W. Fiske, University of Chicago, Chicago, Illinois 60637.

Library of Congress Catalogue Card Number LC 81-48577
International Standard Serial Number ISSN 0271-1249
International Standard Book Number ISBN 87589-912-9

Cover art by Willi Baum
Manufactured in the United States of America

Ordering Information

The paperback sourcebooks listed below are published quarterly and can be ordered either by subscription or as single copies.

Subscriptions cost $35.00 per year for institutions, agencies, and libraries. Individuals can subscribe at the special rate of $21.00 per year *if payment is by personal check.* (Note that the full rate of $35.00 applies if payment is by institutional check, even if the subscription is designated for an individual.) Standing orders are accepted.

Single copies are available at $7.95 when payment accompanies order, and *all single-copy orders under $25.00 must include payment.* (California, Washington, D.C., New Jersey, and New York residents please include appropriate sales tax.) For billed orders, cost per copy is $7.95 plus postage and handling. (Prices subject to change without notice.)

To ensure correct and prompt delivery, all orders must give either the *name of an individual* or an *official purchase order number.* Please submit your order as follows:

Subscriptions: specify series and subscription year.
Single Copies: specify sourcebook code and issue number (such as, MSBS8).

Mail orders for United States and Possessions, Latin America, Canada, Japan, Australia, and New Zealand to:
Jossey-Bass Inc., Publishers
433 California Street
San Francisco, California 94104

Mail orders for all other parts of the world to:
Jossey-Bass Limited
28 Banner Street
London EC1Y 8QE

New Directions for Methodology of Social and Behavioral Science Series
Donald W. Fiske, *Editor-in-Chief*

Contents

Editors' Notes

This volume examines the relationship of various forms of validity to the research process, presents new validity concepts, and re-examines some long-standing issues of convergent and discriminant validation. Two chapters introduce conceptual frameworks. The first locates various forms of validity in relation to one another and in relation to stages of the research process. The second develops a typology of research designs and shows how elements of the typology affect internal, construct, and conclusion validity. The next two chapters present new validity concepts. One analyzes disagreements that may arise between researchers and their subjects about causes and effects; it raises questions about the face validity of conclusion. The other chapter raises questions about the practical validity of effect sizes and shows how effect sizes and significance levels can be combined across independent studies. The last two chapters examine the history and future of the multitrait-multimethod matrix. One places the multitrait-multimethod matrix in the broader context of the reproducibility of research findings. The other explains why the low convergent validity previously reported for personality measures is diluted below what we can assume it truly is.

In the first chapter of this sourcebook, Brinberg and McGrath present a conceptual scheme describing the research process that can be used to organize various traditional forms as well as several new forms of validity. The research process is presented as the interrelationships of conceptual, methodological, and substantive domains. Within this scheme, validity takes on three distinct meanings—value, correspondence, and robustness. This scheme is used to illustrate that many forms of validity are relevant for the research process, to indicate that no single form of validity is the only correct one, and to highlight some underlying features of the different forms of validity.

In the next chapter, Judd and Kenny present a conceptual scheme that describes and organizes a wide range of research designs along five facets: the number of units observed, the number of times that each unit is observed, the number of conditions under which the unit is observed, the combinations of units and conditions (units nested within and crossed with conditions), and the rule used to assign units to conditions (random versus nonrandom assignment). The relationship of construct validity, internal validity, and conclusion validity is then related to this conceptual scheme. In the final section, Judd and Kenny discuss the relative advantages of each form of validity.

In her chapter, Kidder describes a new use for a traditional validity concept. Previously, face validity has been a minimal validity criterion for measurement. Kidder applies it to research conclusions and shows why researchers and subjects may disagree about the face validity of conclusions. Like actors and observers, subjects and researchers occupy different positions and have different perspectives about the causes of subjects' behaviors. Kidder also examines why subjects and researchers may disagree about the effects of events. She concludes with a discussion of research practices that bring researchers' and subjects' perspectives together.

After researchers complete a research project, they are often confronted with the problem of integrating their findings with the conclusions of past research. In his chapter, Rosenthal presents meta-analytic techniques for comparing and combining significance levels and effect sizes of two or more independent studies. He introduces the concept of practical validity in the interpretation of effect size.

In their classic paper, Campbell and Fiske (1959) presented the concepts of convergent and discriminant validity within the context of a multitrait-multimethod strategy. The chapters by Fiske and Campbell in this volume re-examine various aspects of the multitrait-multimethod strategy and present a fresh perspective on its underlying conceptual basis.

Fiske briefly reviews the past twenty years of research on the multitrait-multimethod strategy and relates the concepts of this strategy to other forms of validity. He shows how the multitrait-multimethod approach need not be limited to traits and methods but can include several distinct facets — concepts, measures, populations, times, and analysis models — where any pairwise combination can be used in a multi X–multi Y approach. The remainder of his chapter examines the multitrait-multimethod strategy within the broader context of the reproducibility of findings in research.

Campbell argues that to share a method increases the correspondence between two traits above their true relationship because methods and traits are multiplicatively rather than additively related. In contrast, use of two different methods has the opposite effect of attenuating or diluting the true relationship between traits. Given this relationship between traits and methods, he argues that the low convergence among methods in personality research as well as in other areas may not be as dismal as it initially appears.

David Brinberg
Louise H. Kidder
Editors

Reference

Campbell, D. T., and Fiske, D. W. "Convergent and Discriminant Validation by the Multitrait-Multimethod Matrix." *Psychological Bulletin,* 1959, *30,* 81–105.

David Brinberg is assistant professor in the Department of Textiles and Consumer Economics at the University of Maryland.

Louise H. Kidder is associate professor in the Department of Psychology at Temple University.

Many different forms of validity are organized within a conceptual scheme that describes the research process.

A Network of Validity Concepts Within the Research Process

David Brinberg
Joseph E. McGrath

It will come as no surprise to readers of this chapter that the term *validity* has many uses and many meanings. The methodological literature of our field abounds with terms coined in attempts to assess validity of measurements or validity of relations: *construct validity, convergent validity, predictive validity, face validity, content validity, discriminant validity, internal validity, external validity, statistical conclusion validity*. Each is a useful concept, referring as it does to some particular aspect of the general problem of the validity of research information. Certain other terms as well, such as *reliability* and *generalizability,* are part of a family of validity concepts although they do not include the word *validity*. This chapter presents a conceptual framework that relates all these validity concepts — and others as well — to one another and to the research process. If we can do that successfully, this framework makes it apparent that we need to seek not just one kind of validity in our research endeavors but many, if we are to have high confidence in our body of research findings. We suggest that this framework can help in planning any given study by highlighting the specific validity questions most germane to and most problematic for that study. It can also help in efforts to integrate and to assess the work in a given research area by pointing up the aspects of the overall validity question that represent the most serious limitations of the cumulative work in that area.

D. Brinberg, L. Kidder (Eds.). *New Directions for Methodology of Social and Behavioral Science: Forms of Validity in Research,* no. 12. San Francisco: Jossey-Bass, June 1982.

In the first section of this chapter, we will present a description of the research process that will later serve as a vehicle for considering various aspects of validity. The research enterprise consists of three main stages: a set of prestudy activities that are essential preconditions for the conduct of research of any specific kind, a middle stage that involves conduct of the research study proper and includes three alternate paths for carrying out a two-step research process, and a set of poststudy research activities that are essential before the results can become a useful part of the body of knowledge in a given field.

In the second section of this chapter, we will introduce three general definitions of validity — correspondence, robustness, and value — and we will map these general meanings of validity to the three main portions of the research enterprise as noted above. Correspondence has to do with matters internal to the conduct of a research study, the middle stage, and there are a number of such validity concepts that fit within portions of that process. Robustness has to do with the question of extrapolating beyond any given set of study outcomes — questions of generalizability and external validity — and there are at least three distinct validities involved in this third stage of the research process. Value has to do with the standards and criteria involved in deciding which elements and relations are to provide the substance, concepts, and methods for study; and there are at least three distinct validity-like concepts of this kind involved in stage I, prestudy research activities.

The third section of this chapter is an attempt to draw out some implications of these ways of viewing things — our efforts to answer the "so what" question that lurks, inevitably, in the mind of the reader. Here we will try to describe some similarities between and some distinctions among all of the validities.

The Research Process

Domains, Levels, and Research Paths. We begin by asserting some basic terms. Research involves drawing upon *elements* and *relations* from each of *three domains:* a *conceptual* domain, which includes concepts and relations considered in abstract form; a *methodological* domain, which includes instruments and techniques for obtaining observations and for relating and comparing sets of observations; and a *substantive* domain, which includes states and processes in the real world (events) and sets of relations among events (phenomena).

Any research project is composed of elements and relations from the conceptual, methodological, and substantive domains. Thus, to conduct a research study, it is necessary to bring together elements and relations from all three domains. However, research generally proceeds first by bringing together elements and relations from two of the domains to form a structure, then by bringing elements and relations from the third domain into that structure. Since there are three domains, there are three ways in which one can structure a pair of them. Those three ways represent three distinct research paths, and they pose different opportunities and hazards for the investigator.

First, one can combine elements and relations from the conceptual and methodological domains without bringing in materials from the substantive domain. Such activity involves bringing concepts and relations from the conceptual domain into connection with techniques for assessing concepts and for assessing relations between them. We can regard such concept-method matching as building a *research design* — a plan for doing a study. This matching yields a set of (intended) measures and comparisons (relations). For instance, a researcher could select a particular method or measurement technique, such as the Thurstone scale, to assess a concept, such as attitude. In addition, the researcher can also select a structure, such as factorial design, to assess the relations among the concepts. This concept-method matching, however, is not a study until a particular substantive area is added.

Alternatively, one can begin by combining elements and relations from the conceptual and substantive domains without bringing the methodological domain into the picture. This two-way combination involves mapping concepts onto events and mapping relations between concepts onto relations between events. It results in what we can reasonably call a *theory* — a set of constructs about events and a set of hypotheses about the relations among these constructs. In one instance of this, a researcher selects a particular concept, such as attitude, or a particular set of concepts, such as attitude and social influence, to explain a particular event, such as negative feelings about a political candidate or a particular process such as deciding which candidate to elect. A theory, too, is not yet a study. It has not yet brought in the methodological domain.

A third research path begins by combining elements and relations from the methodological domain with elements and relations from the substantive domain without bringing in materials from the conceptual domain. Such activity involves mapping methods for making observations onto observable events and mapping methods for relating (aggregating, segregating, contrasting, co-relating) sets of observations of events. We can designate such method-substance mapping as construction of a *data set*. For example, a researcher could use a particular method, such as a coding system, to record an event or a process, such as dyadic interaction on a task in order to create a data set. However, this empirical information is not yet a body of evidence until it has been connected to (that is, construed in terms of) some elements and relations from the conceptual domain.

So, along with the three domains from which researchers draw their tools, we have three research structures (combinations of items drawn from two of these domains): designs, theories, and data sets. None of these three structures represents a study, that is, a completion of the research process. Instead, each represents a different way of proceeding in the research process.

In order to complete a research study, we need to carry out a second, completion or integration step. The nature of that step depends on the research structure that has been built in the first step.

When we have built a *research design* by mapping the conceptual onto the methodological domain, we must connect it with the substantive domain. We can think of this as an *implementation* or execution process. For instance, after designing a scaling technique to assess attitudes, a researcher would implement this measure by examining a particular substantive object, such as political candidates. In addition, a researcher could develop a particular design structure, such as factorial design, and complete the research study by implementing the design, that is, by observing a particular process.

When we have built a *theory* by mapping the conceptual onto the substantive domain, we must connect it with the methodological domain. We can think of this as a verification, *theory-testing,* or evaluation process. For example, having developed a theoretical construct, such as attitudes toward political candidates, the researcher would select a particular method, like a sample survey, to test it.

When we have built a body of *data* by mapping the methodological onto the substantive domain, we must connect it with the conceptual domain. We can think of this as an inference, interpretation, or *explanation* process. For example, a researcher examining dyadic interactions selects a set of concepts, such as equity principles, to explain the body of data.

So, we can regard a complete research study as involving one of three patterns: research path A — designing a study, then implementing that design; research path B — developing a theory, then testing that theory; or research path C — collecting and analyzing a set of data, then interpreting those data. Completion of research path A yields an implemented research design, completion of research path B yields a tested theory, and completion of research path C yields an interpreted body of data.

These three products are in one sense the same. That is, they all represent a particular configuration from all three domains. In another sense, they are different. That is, they are arrived at through different sequences of research activities. These three paths are three different styles of research, and they lead the researcher to address three different sets of validity concepts, as we will show later in this chapter. Figure 1 summarizes these three research paths.

The preceding paragraphs have described the different paths for conducting a research study. As researchers, we either build and implement a research design, build and test a theory, or build and interpret a body of data. However, there are some important research activities that occur prior to taking such research paths, and others that occur after completing a study. Here, we will refer to the former as activities of the prestudy stage and to the latter as activities of the poststudy stage.

Figure 1

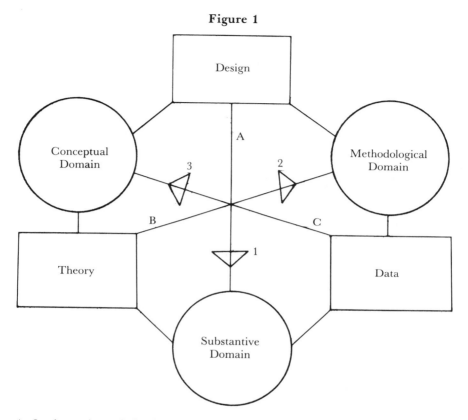

A. Implementing a design by using it on a set of substantive events
B. Testing a theory by evaluating it with an appropriate set of methods
C. Explaining a data set by construing it in terms of a set of concepts

1. Ecological validity
2. Methodological validity
3. Explanatory validity

Prestudy Research Activities. In the present schema, a research study along any one of the three research paths presupposes a prior selection or sampling of elements from the three basic domains. The elements and relations from the substantive domain are the observable events and sets of events that will be studied. In the methodological domain, the elements are methods or strategies for making observations of events, for manipulating and controlling such events, or for both, and the relations are techniques for making comparisons, or exploring relations, among sets of such observed events. In the conceptual domain, elements are concepts, and relations are patterns among such concepts.

However, such selection or sampling from the domains implies that there has been some prior exploration, analysis, or understanding of those domains and of the kinds of elements and relations that can be drawn from them. Such explorations of the three domains are often not regarded as parts of the research process, but they are essential preconditions for execution of research. In the methodological domain, for example, such prestudy exploration leads to the development and use of specific tools — at the level both of methods of measurement, manipulation, and control and of aggregating, comparing, and relating sets of observations. It includes the development of observation instruments or techniques, such as the Minnesota Multiphasic Personality Inventory or the Semantic Differential, and the development of methods for analysis of data, such as three-mode factor analysis, multivariate analysis of variance, and structural equations. In the conceptual domain, prestudy exploration refers to such conceptual developments as the pattern concepts of Gestalt theory, the ideas of intervening variables and goal regions, and the formal properties of a graph theory model. In the substantive domain, prestudy exploration refers to activities carried out by the researcher to get to know the territory. Issues to be considered when exploring the substantive domain include identifying the key events or key properties of the phenomenon and describing the processes underlying the phenomenon.

The importance of these prestudy explorations of the three domains for the network of validity and validity-like concepts will become clearer in the second section of this chapter, where various validity concepts are identified and located within the research process. Here, we will note only that these concepts involve the values or criteria used in deciding what aspects of these domains to sample. These values or criteria most often are derived from the prevailing paradigm (Kuhn, 1962); occasionally, they reflect the introduction of a new paradigm. They are used to decide what the substantive events and processes are, to identify useful concepts and conceptual patterns, and to develop effective methods for observation and analysis. All these sets of decisions are pertinent to a broadly construed network of validity concepts, although they are not necessarily relevant to validity in a narrowly defined sense. An instance of a value or criterion in social science research today is the use of significance testing to evaluate and to identify statistically significant empirical patterns. Inferences that are made from such patterns without reference to such criteria are generally considered not valid; that is, as not true or not important.

Poststudy Research Activities. After any research path is completed, some further crucial activities — here called poststudy activities — must be carried out before the results of that study can become useful knowledge. These poststudy activities are different for the three different research paths.

In research path A, the first step involves building a design, and the second step involves gathering sets of observations from the substantive domain in the pattern called for by that design. When such a study is completed, the researcher still faces a key problem: the extent to which results would hold up for other samples of substantive observations. This is the problem of generalizability or robustness of findings. It is one form of external validity. These matters will be discussed further in the second section of this chapter.

In research path B, the first step involves building a theory, and the second step involves testing the constructs and hypotheses of that theory by bringing some methods of observation and comparison to bear on them. When such a study is completed, the researcher still faces a key problem: the extent to which results would hold up for other sets of methods. This is the problem of the degree to which findings are independent of methods of study. It is another aspect of external validity.

In research path C, the first step involves constructing a set of data, and the second step involves bringing conceptual elements and relations to bear on these data in order to explain or interpret them. When such a study is completed, the researcher still faces a key problem: whether alternative sets of concepts would explain the data equally well. This is the problem of the explanatory power of the conceptualizations. It is a third aspect of external validity.

In effect, all three of these poststudy research activities involve problems of selection or sampling of substantive observations, of methods, and of concepts, respectively — and all three are variations of the general concept of external validity, generalization, or robustness. All have to do with the usefulness of findings beyond the specific evidence of a specific study. All imply that elements and relations from one of the domains are somehow resampled. These three research activities thus tie.back, in some interesting ways, to the stages of the research paths by which the research study was conducted.

Forms of Validity Within the Research Process

Various Meanings of Validity. As we noted at the start, the reader is certainly aware that the term *validity* has been used in juxtaposition with a number of modifiers: *construct* validity, *face* validity, *predictive* validity, *internal* validity, and the like. The reader is also aware that a number of familiar terms within the methodological literature, such as *reliability* and *generalizability,* are closely related to the validity concepts. What we wish to establish here is a systematic ordering of such validity and validity-like concepts in relation to one another and in relation to parts of the research process so that the full power of those concepts and the relations among them can be more clearly seen. One side effect — a beneficial one, we would argue — is that such an analysis will identify gaps within the schema for which there is no readily familiar validity term. New validity terms and concepts can be developed to fill those gaps.

Table 1 summarizes the various validities within the three stages of the research process.

All these validity and validity-like terms share several underlying meanings. One meaning, upon which we will place major emphasis, is the idea of *validity as correspondence*. Many of the validity terms mentioned here and in the literature hinge on the key idea of correspondence between two sets of things, whether they be two sets of constructs, a set of concepts and a set of observations, two sets of measures, or something else. The idea of validity as correspondence will guide us in our discussion of the validities associated with the paths involved in stage II research studies (as distinct from the prestudy and poststudy research activities).

Another central idea of validity has to do with dependability, generalizability, or *robustness*. One set of validity concepts — those related to external validity for the most part — have to do with the degree to which a set of concepts or findings will hold up when extrapolated, or generalized, or extended to materials not yet brought under research inquiry. This is the meaning of validity that we will use for the poststudy research activities.

There is still a third meaning of validity, more often implied in lay uses of the term than in technical uses made by researchers. Sometimes, when people say, "That's not valid" or ask, "But is your test valid?" what they mean to ask is, "Is your evidence really true?" They are asking about its truth value in some fundamental, epistemological sense. These uses suggest a third meaning of validity, which is consistent with the word form itself; namely, *validity as value*. This is the meaning of the term that is most applicable to what we have called the prestudy research activities. When one explores and clarifies the substantive domain, preparatory to selection of events and phenomena for observation and study, it is in the interest of identifying events and phenomena that are both real, or true, and important. Similarly, when one explores the conceptual domain, it is in search of concepts and relations that are worthy of study, and when one explores the methodological domain, it is in search of methods and procedures that are valuable for research use.

We have, then, three fundamental meanings of the term *validity*, and we map them onto the three major portions of the research endeavor. For prestudy research activities, which explore and clarify the three domains, we must be concerned with criteria or standards — with values used in identification and selection of elements and relations. For research activities in the conduct of a research study proper, no matter which of the three research paths is followed in conducting the study, we must be concerned with correspondences among a number of sets of elements and relations among the three domains. For poststudy research activities, we must be concerned with the robustness or generalizability of the meanings inferred from study outcomes. We will talk about these three sets of validities in more detail in the paragraphs to follow, beginning with the second stage of the research process.

Table 1. A Network of Validities Within the Research Process

Stage I: Prior Validities: Validity as Value	Path	Stage II: Internal Validities: Validity as Correspondence		Stage III: External Validities: Validity as Robustness
		Logical Validities	*Integration Validities*	
			Implement	
	A. *Design*	Element: Instrument validity	Element: Instrument use validity	1. *Ecological Validity* (repeated sampling of the substantive domain)
		Relation: Comparison validity	Relation: Execution validity	
Rules of evidence and standards for sampling from the conceptual, methodological, and substantive domains.			*Test*	
	B. *Theory*	Element: Construct validity	Element: Operational validity	2. *Methodological Validity* (repeated sampling of the methodological domain)
		Relation: Hypothesis validity	Relation: Predictive validity	
			Explain	
	C. *Data*	Element: Reliability	Element: Inferential reliability	3. *Explanatory Validity* (repeated sampling of the conceptual domain)
		Relation: Descriptive statistical validity	Relation: Inferential statistical validity	

Validities Internal to the Research Process. The second stage of the research enterprise, the part we have called the *research process proper,* consists of three alternate paths, each with two major steps. For each path, the first step consists of a structuring activity: relating elements and relations from two of the domains. The validity issues associated with this step may be termed *logical validities.* These validity issues can be evaluated prior to conduct of the research study. The second step consists of relating that structure, which is based on two domains, to elements and relations from the third domain. The validity issues associated with this step may be termed *integration validities.* These are validity issues involved in carrying out a research study. Therefore, there are four validities within each path: there is a correspondence, at both the element and the relations levels, within the structure built from the first two domains; and there is a correspondence, at both the element and relations levels, between that structure and the third domain. Two stages, by two levels, by three paths, yield a total of twelve validities. All twelve might reasonably be called *internal validities,* in the sense that they are internal to the ongoing research process within a study. (See the center section of Table 1.)

The first step of research path A involves the development of a study design from elements and relations in the conceptual and methodological domains. The matching of concepts and methods at the element level yields a set of intended measures. The correspondence between the methods and concepts may simply be termed *instrument validity,* that is, the extent to which a measure can correspond with (that is, assess) a concept or set of concepts.

One major threat to the validity of an instrument is the potential confounding between the instrument and the theoretical concepts. Use of a multitrait-multimethod approach (Campbell and Fiske, 1959) makes it possible to separate the variation associated with a particular method, that is, method variance, from the variance associated with the theoretical concepts, that is, convergent and discriminant validity.

In the matching of concepts and methods at the relations level lie the correspondence concerns that Campbell and his associates have called *internal validity.* Note, first, that in this chapter, we are using the term *internal validities* to refer to the whole set of twelve validity concepts within the three research paths of stage II, rather than just to the specific path, step, or level validity considered here. Note, second, that our use is close to that of the original formulation by Campbell and Stanley (1966), which listed seven main classes of threats. In a more recent presentation, Cook and Campbell (1979) have described some additional threats to internal validity that are related here to the validities of the second step of path A, at the relations level. To avoid confusion of terms, we will use a new label for the correspondence between conceptual relations and methodological relations within the study design. While logical validity, inferential validity, or causal validity are all appropriate, we will use the term *comparison validity.* The central notion has to do with the extent to which planned comparisons within the study will permit clear inferences about the logical relation among the variables involved.

Numerous researchers, including Campbell and Stanley (1966), Cook and Campbell (1979) and Runkel and McGrath (1972), have discussed a wide set of factors that potentially confound the interpretation of findings resulting from a particular experimental design. Factors often regarded as defining classes of plausible rival hypotheses will not be elaborated here. The reader who is interested in a detailed discussion of these threats to internal (that is, comparison) validity should read the sources cited in our references. In addition to these familiar threats to comparison validity (such as history, maturation, and instrumentation), other characteristics of designs need also to be considered. The way in which a set of concepts is structured will affect the validity of a research conclusion. For instance, several researchers (including Greenwald, 1976) have discussed the relative advantages and disadvantages of within-subject and between-subjects designs. Different assumptions are required for these two types of designs (for example, regarding carry-over effects, lack of exposure to the range of the stimuli, and the like). These, too, bear on the validity of the design for any particular research study.

Some potential threats to the validity of a design stem from nonrandom assignment of subjects within the design structure. Cook and Campbell (1979) have distinguished between experimental (random assignment) and quasi-experimental (nonrandom assignment) designs and have pointed out factors that need to be considered to reach valid inferences from these two types of design.

The correspondences involved in the theory structure (of step one of research path B) have been termed *construct validity.* Cook and Campbell (1979) use that term at the element level. They talk of the construct validity of the cause and the construct validity of the effect. Earlier Cronbach and Meehl (1955) used the term to describe the correspondence involved in fitting a construct within a nomological net; hence, they use the term at the relations level. Here, we will refer to these two theoretical validities as *construct validity* for the element level and as *hypothesis validity* for the relations level.

Cook and Campbell (1979) describe several threats to the correspondence of the theoretical concept and the event. For instance, inadequate specification of the theoretical concept can reduce its correspondence with a particular event. Harris (1976) deals with this issue in his review of several qualitative theories and discusses the difficulty in providing an adequate test for an inadequately specified theory. Cook and Campbell (1979) offer a good example of this potential confound from the area of attitude research. In addition to inadequate specification, the functional relationship between the concept and the event can be misspecified. For instance, a theoretical concept can be treated as continuous (as in the usual treatment of the attitude concept), but the set of events under observation can actually be categorical (that is, people may view events of a particular class as either good or bad). Such lack of correspondence between the concept and event reduces the validity of the construct.

For research path C, the correspondence involved in the first step (the structured body of data) has to do with the mapping of methods (of observation, manipulation, and control at the element level and of aggregating, comparing, and relating at the relation level) onto events and phenomena in the substantive domain. At the element level, such correspondence has to do with the reliability (that is, with the internal consistency, stability, or equivalence) of the set of measurements used to generate data about a variable. At the relations level, the correspondence has to do with what Cook and Campbell (1979) call *statistical conclusion validity*. Only a part of what Cook and Campbell include in statistical conclusion validity is included here (that is, the part analogous to descriptive statistics); we will treat the rest (that is, the part analogous to inferential statistics) as part of the validity that we associate with the second step of this research path.

The major threat to obtaining a reliable measure is measurement error. Many factors can increase unreliability (for example, inconsistency among coders, changes in the interviewer, fatigue of respondent or observer). A detailed discussion of these and other factors can be found in any standard psychometric text (for example, Guilford, 1954; Nunnally, 1967). Potential threats to statistical conclusion validity include violations of underlying assumptions (for example, normality, uncorrelated error) as well as incorrect specification of the function that underlies an event. For instance, if the underlying relation between proximity and friendship is nonlinear, use of a linear model will not fully describe their relationship.

The second step of each of these three research paths involves connecting elements and relations from a third domain with the structure built from elements and relations of the other two domains. These integration validities (column B of Table 1) involve correspondences between the elements and relations of that third domain and the terms of the two-domain structure with which they are to be connected. For research path A, where a study design is to be connected to elements and relations from the substantive domain, the correspondences have to do ·with the execution of the design as intended. Cook and Campbell (1979), for example, discuss several threats (to internal validity, in their usage) that have to do with imperfections not in the planning of a design but in its execution. For example, they talk about several ways in which the experimental treatment, intended only for the experimental group, can affect cases intended to be in a comparison or control group. They point out that these threats to internal validity cannot be avoided by randomization. Of course, numerous factors can influence the implementation of a design. These factors include demand characteristics and experimenter biases (that is, cues, to which the subject attends, that are incidental to the main emphasis of the research), and subject roles (that is, the orientation that a subject adopts when responding in an experimental setting). When a researcher implements a design, these factors need to be considered in addition to the many threats to internal (that is, comparison) validity of the design. Similarly, some features of instrument validity apply in the execution of the study design. For instance, the orientation that a respondent takes to a particular instrument (for example, response set) can influence the validity of the instrument's use. We will call these second-step validities *execution validity* at the relations level and *validity of instrument use* at the element level.

For research path B, where a theory is to be connected with a set of methods for making observations, the correspondence involved has to do with how well the chosen methods operationalize the theory. We can reasonably call this *operational validity* at the element level and *predictive validity* at the relations level.

For research path C, where a body of data is to be explained by connecting it with a set of concepts and conceptual relations, the correspondence involved has to do with the degree to which the concepts and relations account for or explain the body of data. This correspondence involves the inferential aspects of a measure's reliability and of a relation's statistical conclusion validity. For instance, suppose that a researcher wants to determine whether two proposed measures assess the same or different conceptual dimensions. One strategy would be to place each measure in a regression analysis predicting some criterion. If both measures received a significant regression weight, the researcher could conclude that each measured separate conceptual dimensions. However, several researchers (for example, Birnbaum and Mellers, 1979; Brewer, Campbell, and Crano, 1970) have pointed out that this inference can be misleading, since two measures that are imperfect measurements of the same underlying conceptual dimension can both receive significant regression weights. The key point for the present discussion is that the assumptions of a statistical technique will influence the inferences made concerning theoretical concepts. Since the correspondence between elements and relations from the conceptual domain with a body of data both involve inferential validities, they might reasonably be called the inferential reliability of a measure and the inferential statistical validity of a relation.

We have, thus far, identified and labelled a dozen validities within the research process proper, one for each of the two levels and two steps of each research path within this main, middle stage of the research enterprise. These terms are arrayed in Table 1. All of them, collectively, may be regarded as internal validities dealing with correspondences within the research process. In the succeeding paragraphs, we will describe certain validity-related concepts that deal with values on the one hand and with robustness or generalizability on the other. In the last section of this chapter, we will consider some implications of the whole schema.

Validities External to the Research Process Proper: Poststudy Validities. When a study has been completed, in that the two steps of one of the research paths have been carried out — which, presumably, means that the four internal validities involved in that path have been dealt with adequately — the investigator is still faced with certain important problems. The specific formulation of the problem depends on the path that has been followed. For each path, the problem is a different aspect of what might be called *external validity*. In all three cases, the problem has to do with the import that study results will have for some body of knowledge external to the specific study. All three forms of external validity are necessary for researchers to have confidence in their conclusions.

For research path A, in which a design is built and then implemented, the key problem facing the investigator has to do with the degree to which the sample of observations in the study represents the substantive domain. This is the question of the *ecological validity* of the set of observations, hence of the study's findings. It is one aspect of external validity.

For research path B, in which a theory is built and then tested, the key problem facing the investigator has to do with the degree to which the findings are particular to the set of methods chosen to test the theory. This is the question of generalizability over methods or *methodological validity*. It is a second aspect of external validity.

For research path C, in which a body of data is built and then explained, the key problem facing the investigator has to do with the degree to which the chosen concepts account for the study findings. That is, the investigator must explore whether there are alternative, equally plausible, conceptual explanations for the findings. This is the question of *explanatory validity*. It is a third aspect of external validity, although it is not usually thought of as such.

So, completion of each of the three research paths, even with resolution of the four internal validities involved in each path, still leaves one of three external validity problems to be dealt with. In each case, the essence of the external validity problem is the question of sampling — the extent to which the findings can be expected to generalize over substantive, methodological, or conceptual elements and relations not yet studied. It was noted at the beginning of this chapter that one meaning of the word *validity* is dependability or robustness. These external validities are not so much questions of correspondence as questions of the generalizability or robustness of findings.

Validity-Related Matters in Prestudy Research Activities. The prestudy research activities discussed in the previous paragraphs involve exploring and clarifying each of the three domains. Deciding what elements and relations to sample from the substantive domain, for example, implies deciding what aspects of that domain will be regarded as real and important events and processes. Similarly, for the methodological domain and for the conceptual domain, sampling implies deciding what elements and relations will be regarded as important and legitimate. In all three cases, applying criteria and standards to decide what elements and relations will be regarded as real implies applying a set of values to such selections. These values are validity-like, but they are neither correspondence nor robustness. We term them *prior validities*.

It is interesting to note that paradigm shifts are often shifts in the sets of values or criteria involved in establishing the elements and relations of a domain that will be regarded as real and worthy of use. The Gestalt movement, for example, challenged concepts that had been used for interpreting human learning and substituted new elements and relations from the conceptual domain. In contrast, development of methods for significance testing, or observation instruments like MMPI, or techniques for applying experimental methods in a certain area represent shifts in paradigm from within the methodological domain. Finally, one can make a case that the Freudian revolution represented a shift in paradigm within the substantive domain. Freud pointed to new elements and relations (for example, unconscious forces, repression, and other mechanisms) that were to be regarded as the important events and phenomena. He thereby shifted the definition of what was real and important within the substantive domain. The reader interested in a more detailed discussion of the influence of culture and values on the research process should read Gergen (1973) and Kaplan (1964).

Implications

Besides needing various techniques, strategies, and methods for conducting research, the sophisticated behavioral scientist, we would argue, also needs an underlying framework for understanding the research process. In this chapter, we have presented such a framework. This framework identifies the key components of research (elements and relations from conceptual, methodological, and substantive domains); indicates how these domains can be combined (by forming a design, a theory, or a body of data); describes three different paths for conducting a research project (by implementing a design, testing a theory, or explaining a body of data); and explores how one can assess the robustness of research findings (by considering whether the findings generalize across events or processes from the substantive domain, across methods from the methodological domain, or across concepts from the conceptual domain). We believe that this framework can be used to illuminate the various forms of validity, the interrelationships among these forms, and the relations of these validities to the research process.

Three basic definitions of validity — validity as values, validity as correspondence, and validity as robustness — are mapped onto the three stages of research. Each of these three definitions is appropriate for describing one stage of the research process. Previously defined validities (for example, construct validity, convergent validity, discriminant validity), as well as several new validity terms (for example, instrument use validity, hypothesis validity) are located within the conceptual framework. Rather than simply adding to the plethora of validity concepts, however, we have located the new validity concepts along with the familiar concepts in an integrated framework for describing the research process.

Finally, the framework highlights the need for considering several forms of validity when conducting any research project and that the particular types of validity that need to be considered vary as a function of the research path selected. For instance, if a researcher forms a design and then implements that design, the forms of validity associated with the design (instrument and comparison validity) and with its implementation (instrument use and execution validity) need to be considered. In addition to these validities, the researchers need to address the issue of the robustness of the findings for successive samples of substantive events (the ecological validity of the results). The theory research path or the data research path would pose a different set of validity questions.

The framework also poses certain problems, to be sure, and the approach itself courts some hazards. When one proffers a complex and comprehensive conceptual framework, such as this one, there is always a risk that accuracy will be traded off for elegance. We recognize that a reasonable case can be made for other constructions of the research process and for other distinctions and relations among validity concepts. We offer here one set of such concepts and relations. It is a set, we hope, that will help to inform future research.

References

Birnbaum, M. H., and Mellers, B. A. "Stimulus Recognition May Mediate Exposure Effects." *Journal of Personality and Social Psychology,* 1979, *37,* 391–394.

Brewer, M. B., Campbell, D. T., and Crano, W. B. "Testing a Single Factor Model as an Alternative to the Misuse of Partial Correlations in Hypothesis Testing." *Sociometry,* 1970, *33,* 1–11.

Campbell, D. T., and Fiske, D. W. "Convergent and Discriminant Validation by the Multitrait-Multimethod Matrix." *Psychological Bulletin,* 1959, *30,* 81–105.

Campbell, D. T., and Stanley, J. C. *Experimental and Quasi-Experimental Designs for Research.* Chicago: Rand McNally, 1966.

Cook, T. D., and Campbell, D. T. *Design and Analysis of Quasi Experiments for Field Settings.* Chicago: Rand McNally, 1979.

Cronbach, L. J., and Meehl, P. E. "Construct Validity in Psychological Tests." *Psychological Bulletin,* 1955, *52,* 281–302.

Gergen, K. J. "Social Psychology as History." *Journal of Personality and Social Psychology,* 1973, *26,* 309–320.

Greenwald, A. G. "Within-Subject Designs: To Use or Not to Use?" *Psychological Bulletin,* 1976, *83,* 314–320.

Guilford, J. P. *Psychometric Methods.* New York: McGraw-Hill, 1954.

Harris, R. J. "The Uncertain Connections Between Verbal Theories and Research Hypotheses in Social Psychology." *Journal of Experimental Social Psychology,* 1976, *12,* 210–219.

Kaplan, A. *The Conduct of Inquiry.* Scranton, Pa.: Chandler, 1964.

Kuhn, T. S. *The Structure of Scientific Revolutions.* Chicago: University of Chicago Press, 1962.

Nunnally, J. C. *Psychometric Theory.* New York: McGraw-Hill, 1967.

Runkel, P. J., and McGrath, J. E. *Research on Human Behavior: A Systematic Guide to Method.* New York: Holt, Rinehart and Winston, 1972.

David Brinberg is assistant professor in the Department of Textiles and Consumer Economics at the University of Maryland.

Joseph E. McGrath is professor of psychology at the University of Illinois, Urbana.

*A framework for organizing research designs
is related to various forms of validity.*

Research Design and Research Validity

*Charles M. Judd
David A. Kenny*

The purpose of this chapter is to examine how the use of various research designs affects research validity. To do this, we must define research validity. The first section of the chapter is devoted to this task. We must also discriminate among research designs, making distinctions that both define specific designs and are relevant to research validity. The second section of the chapter is devoted to that task. Only after we have defined research validity and distinguished research designs can we relate the latter to the former. This is what we do in the third section of the chapter. In the fourth and final section, we examine the consequences for research validity of incorrect definition of the research design; that is, of acting as if the data had been collected under a different design from the one actually used.

Research Validity

In a general sense, research validity can best be defined as the informativeness of a specific study for the development and support of hypotheses.

Support for this chapter was provided in part from National Science Foundation grant BNS 8005737 to the first author and BNS 7913820 to the second.

D. Brinberg, L. Kidder (Eds.). *New Directions for Methodology of Social and Behavioral Science: Forms of Validity in Research*, no. 12. San Francisco: Jossey-Bass, June 1982.

Traditionally, two specific types of research validity have been defined: internal validity and external validity (Campbell and Stanley, 1963.) Internal validity has generally been defined as the extent to which the observed treatment effect in a study is causal. External validity has been referred to as the issue of generalizability: To what populations and settings can the results of a study be generalized?

Recently, two other sorts of research validity have been added to the list (Cook and Campbell, 1979; Judd and Kenny, 1981). Construct validity (Cronbach and Meehl, 1955) refers to the extent to which the independent and dependent variables in a study successfully represent the intended theoretical constructs. Conclusion validity has been defined as the extent to which the statistical conclusions of a study are accurate. Specifically, it addresses the question of whether a research design is sufficiently precise or powerful to enable us to detect a relationship between the independent and dependent variables, should one exist.

For the purposes of this chapter, the four research validities just identified — internal validity, external validity, construct validity, and conclusion validity — can be reduced to three once we realize that external validity and construct validity both refer to generalizations from a study to theoretical phenomena of interest. Classically, external validity has referred to generalizations from samples to populations — to what extent do samples represent the population? — and construct validity has referred to generalizations from variables to theoretical constructs — to what extent do variables represent the constructs of interest? In both cases, we are concerned with the ability of a study to address the theoretical phenomena of a research hypothesis. We want to know whether we can generalize the results of a study to the population, setting, treatment construct, and outcome construct that are of theoretical interest. Because both external validity and construct validity refer to generalizations from indicators or from specific operationalizations to theoretical phenomena of interest, it makes sense to collapse them into a single research validity. Instead of inventing a new term to refer to the ability to generalize from the research to theoretical phenomena, we will continue to use the term *construct validity*. As it is used here, however, construct validity refers to the ability to generalize from the research variables, sample, and setting to the the constructs, populations, and settings of theoretical interest.

Elsewhere (Judd and Kenny, 1981), we have used the term *external validity* to refer to generalizations from constructs and populations operationalized in the research to other constructs and populations. When external validity is used in this sense, construct validity refers to generalizations from the research to the theoretical phenomena that were operationalized, while external validity concerns generalizations to other theoretical phenomena. However, decisions about research design are of little relevance to external validity construed in this sense, so the latter term will not be used in the rest of this chapter.

With this discussion behind us, we propose the following working definitions for the research validities. Construct validity is the extent to which the theoretical treatment, outcome, population, and setting have been successfully operationalized in the research. Conclusion validity is the extent to which the research design is sufficiently precise or powerful to detect a relationship between the independent and dependent variables, should one exist. Internal validity is the extent to which the detected relationship between the independent and dependent variables is causal or the extent to which detected treatment effects are not due to other competing causes.

Research Designs

Now that the various types of validity have been defined, we turn our attention to research designs. In its most basic form, research involves the observation of some number of units under some number of conditions. This very general definition requires elaboration. By *units,* we mean whatever is observed. Typically, units are individuals, and we will frequently refer to them as *individuals* or *subjects.* Units need not be individuals, however, since research can be done on families, communities, and so forth. For the time being, a unit is whatever emits a response of interest, regardless of its apparent level of aggregation. By *conditions,* we refer to the levels of what is traditionally called the *independent variable.* The conditions specify the treatments under which observations are taken. Sometimes, they are fabricated by the researcher, but they do not need to be.

Research designs differ in four respects: in the number of conditions used, in the way in which units and conditions are combined, in the number of units observed, and in the number of times that units are observed. These four distinctions are discussed in the following paragraphs.

Often, only a single condition is studied. For instance, an instructor can distribute a questionnaire to students in the class in order to evaluate his or her effectiveness. All students in the class are in the same condition. Much more frequently, however, observations are gathered from units under a variety of conditions. We observe subjects in a crowded or an uncrowded room in order to infer responses to crowding. We examine differences in voting patterns among different religious groups. We evaluate a counseling program by observing individuals who are being counseled and individuals who are not. In all these examples, observations are taken in different conditions.

Whenever a study uses multiple conditions, researchers wish to compare the responses of subjects across these conditions. Such comparisons can be of two sorts. Researchers can compare either the responses of different subjects in different conditions or the responses of the same subjects in different conditions. In the language of experimental design, units can be nested within conditions, or they can be crossed with conditions. To illustrate the distinction, suppose we conduct a study to evaluate different teaching techniques. We can observe all students under each of the different learning conditions, or we can assign different students to each of the different learning conditions. To illustrate the distinction again, if we are interested in the effects of age on cognitive abilities, we can observe children of different ages, or we can observe the same children at several different times as they grow.

Regardless of whether subjects are nested within conditions or crossed with conditions, we may wish to gather responses from only a single subject within each condition or from multiple subjects in every condition. This distinction closely corresponds to the difference between single-subject research designs ($N = 1$) and multiple-subject designs, except that we are referring to the number of subjects within conditions, rather than to the number of subjects overall.

Regardless of the number of conditions and of the number of subjects within each condition, research designs differ also in the number of times that any given subject is observed or measured in any given condition. Either we may take many observations on a subject within a condition, or we may take only a single observation. The number of observations from a subject within a condition is called the *number of replications*. When subjects are nested within conditions, the number of replications equals the total number of times that any subject is observed. When subjects are crossed within conditions, the total number of observations from any subject equals the number of replications times the number of conditions.

To summarize the preceding paragraphs, we have presented four distinctions among research designs, depending, first, on whether the number of conditions (k) is equal to or greater than one; second, on whether units are nested within conditions or crossed with conditions (this distinction is relevant only when there are multiple conditions); third, on whether the number of units per condition (n) is equal to or greater than one; and fourth, on whether the number of replications (r) is equal to or greater than one. By combining these four distinctions, we obtain the matrix of possible research designs presented in Table 1. The rows of this matrix refer both to the number of conditions and to nesting of units within conditions versus crossing of units with conditions. The columns of the matrix refer to the number of units within any condition and to the number of replications. In the cells of the matrix, we present formulas representing the total number of observations (*Obs*) and the total number of units observed (*N*) within the research design defined by the cell. To clarify, we discuss some frequently used designs in the paragraphs following.

Table 1. Research Design Distinctions

	Multiple Units within Conditions		Single Unit within Conditions	
	Multiple Replications (r > 1)	No Replications (r = 1)	Multiple Replications (r > 1)	No Replications (r = 1)
Multiple Conditions (k > 1)				
Units Nested within Conditions	Obs = Nr N = kn	Obs = N N = kn	Obs = kr N = k	Obs = k N = k
Units Crossed with Conditions	Obs = Nkr N = n	Obs = Nk N = n	Obs = kr N = 1	Obs = k N = 1
Single Conditions (k = 1)	Obs = Nr N = n	Obs = N N = n	Obs = r N = 1	Obs = 1 N = 1

N refers to the total number of units observed.
Obs refers to the total number of observations.
n refers to the number of units per condition.
r refers to the number of replications.
k refers to the number of conditions.

One research design that is occasionally used in evaluating social interventions is the design in the upper left-hand cell of the matrix. In such a design, different subjects are in different conditions (frequently, there is a treatment group and a control group), numerous subjects are observed under any condition, and each is observed multiple times; that is, there are multiple replications. For instance, in the New Jersey negative income tax experiment, families were assigned to different income maintenance levels, and then their work habits were observed repeatedly (Rees, 1974).

Many experiments in psychology use the design defined by the cell in the second column and second row of the matrix. In this design, numerous subjects are each observed a single time in each condition. Suppose we were doing a study on the recall of verbal material to see whether recall varied as a function of information complexity. It would be quite reasonable to expose each of N subjects to both complex and noncomplex information (probably in different orders) and test their recall after each exposure.

Anthropological research frequently studies groups by observing them in their native habitat over an extended period of time. Such a research procedure employs the design defined by the cell in the third row and third column of the matrix. Here, a single unit, the group, is repeatedly observed under relatively unchanging conditions.

The interrupted time series design has been used in a variety of settings. This design is defined by the cell in the second row and third column of the matrix. Here, a single unit is observed repeatedly under each condition. In the best-known example, traffic fatalities in the state of Connecticut were monitored for months prior to and after the imposition of a statewide crackdown on speeding (Ross and Campbell, 1968). In this research, the unit was the state, and observations were gathered from that unit over time. Some of these observations were gathered during the crackdown, and others were gathered in years when there was no crackdown. Hence, the same unit was observed repeatedly in two different conditions.

Finally, political polls and surveys are a ubiquitous form of research. Pollsters interview many different respondents a single time in many different naturally occurring conditions. Such surveys use the design defined by the cell in the first row and second column of the matrix. For instance, to learn whether presidential preference varies with religion, we would ask multiple voters (units) of different religions (conditions) about their preferred candidate.

A Fifth Distinction: Assignment Rule. We have not yet mentioned one of the distinctions most frequently made among research designs, that is, the distinction between experimental and nonexperimental designs (Campbell and Stanley, 1963).

Whenever the number of conditions exceeds one, as in the top and middle rows of the matrix in Table 1, we can distinguish among research designs by the procedure that determines the condition under which any given observation is taken. Independent of whether subjects are nested within conditions or crossed with conditions, there is some rule or procedure that determines assignment to conditions. This rule or procedure is known as the *assignment rule*. Different sorts of assignment rule result in different research designs.

There are three major types of assignment rule (Judd and Kenny, 1981.) The first, a random assignment rule, is used in randomized experimental research designs. Under this rule, units or observations are randomly assigned to conditions. In nonexperimental designs, the assignment rule, by definition, is not random; however, it may be known. Thus, under the second type of assignment rule, the researcher knows exactly what variable has determined the condition under which any particular observation is taken. Under the third type of assignment rule, the researcher does not know exactly what factor determines the condition under which any particular observation is taken.

All three types of assignment rule can be found in the eight research designs defined by the top and middle rows of the matrix in Table 1. To clarify this, we have reproduced the top and middle rows of Table 1 in Table 2, adding the additional distinction of type of assignment rule. The third row of Table 1 has been omitted, because when there is only a single condition, we cannot meaningfully speak of an assignment rule.

When units are nested within conditions, that is, when different units are observed in each of the different conditions, the assignment rule refers to the procedure by which units are assigned to conditions. When units are crossed with conditions, the assignment rule refers to the procedure by which observations are assigned to conditions. For instance, if we were comparing the effects of two school curricula, and subjects were nested within conditions, the assignment rule would determine which subjects were taught under which curriculum. If subjects were crossed with conditions, every subject would be exposed to and tested in every condition, so the assignment rule would determine the order in which subjects were exposed to or observed under the various curricula.

To facilitate discussion of the designs defined by Table 2, we will break the matrix into quadrants. These quadrants are identified by the letters that appear in the cells of Table 2. In the six cells of quadrant A, each subject is in only one condition, and there are multiple subjects in each condition. In this quadrant, a random assignment rule gives rise to the type of randomized experiment used widely in social-psychological and evaluation research. In the typical social-psychological experiment, subjects arrive in the laboratory and are randomly assigned to one treatment condition or another.

The use of a known assignment rule in this quadrant defines a quasi-experimental design known as the regression-discontinuity design (Thistlethwaite and Campbell, 1960). In this design, units are assigned to a given treatment condition on the basis of some known criterion. For instance, Sea-

Table 2. Further Research Design Distinctions

Multiple Conditions (k > 1)	Assignment Rule	Multiple Units within Conditions		Single Unit within Conditions	
		Multiple Replications	No Replications	Multiple Replications	No Replications
Units Nested within Conditions	Random	A	A	B	B
	Known	A	A	B	B
	Unknown	A	A	B	B
Units Crossed with Conditions	Random	C	C	D	D
	Known	C	C	D	D
	Unknown	C	C	D	D

ver and Quarton (1973) used this design to evaluate the effect on students' subsequent performance of their being placed on the dean's list. Assignment to the two conditions (on the dean's list or not on the dean's list) was determined by prior grades. The use of an *unknown* assignment rule in this quadrant produces two types of design, depending upon whether pretreatment information on the units is available to the researcher. If such information is available, the archetypal quasiexperiment results: the nonequivalent control group design. Such a design has been used repeatedly in evaluating social interventions in which assignment has not been controlled by the researcher (for example, Ball and Bogatz, 1970; Hardin and Borus, 1971). If no pretreatment information on the units is available, use of an unknown assignment rule in this quadrant results in a correlational research design. This design, which Campbell and Stanley (1963) called a *static group comparison design,* is the design employed in most surveys. For instance, different survey respondents respond under different conditions (for example, their religion or income level), but the researcher is not entirely aware of the complex processes that have caused individual respondents to be in their respective condition. In addition, no data are collected on respondents prior to their being in that condition.

In designs in quadrant B of Table 2, each unit is only in one condition, and there is only a single unit in each condition. These research designs are not very useful. In these designs, units are totally confounded with conditions. We will return to this point in the next section of this chapter.

Nevertheless, it is still possible to discriminate among these designs according to the type of assignment rule. Under a random rule, each of the units is randomly assigned to a condition. Under a known rule, we know why each unit is in the condition that it is in. Finally, under an unknown rule, we do not know the factors that account for condition assignment.

In the designs of quadrant C of Table 2, every unit is observed in every condition, and there are multiple units. Since the assignment rule determines the condition under which any observation is taken, it determines the order in which each unit is exposed to the various conditions. When the number of replications is one, a random rule is equivalent to random assignment of units to different sequences of condition exposure. Such a design is commonly known as a *repeated measures experimental design;* in this design, sequence is determined randomly. When the replications are multiple, the different sequences of condition exposure include exposure to each condition a number of times in randomly determined orders.

In this quadrant, a known assignment rule defines designs in which the researcher knows the factor or factors responsible for any given observation's being taken under any given condition. In essence, this amounts to knowing what accounts for the order in which a unit is exposed to the various conditions. Under an unknown assignment rule, the researcher does not control the sequence of condition exposure, and the researcher is also unaware of the factors responsible for it.

In quadrant D of Table 2, only a single unit is observed in research and it is exposed to each condition either once or repeatedly. If there are no replications, the number of observations equals the number of conditions, which results in the confounding of condition and order of exposure. Hence, while it is possible to discriminate among assignment rules (for example, a randomly determined order), it serves little purpose to do so. However, when there are numerous replications, the assignment rule distinctions become quite important.

Under a random rule, the single unit is observed repeatedly under each condition. In addition, the unit goes into and out of the various conditions in a random manner. Such a design involves a time series data structure, in which the various conditions are unconfounded with order or time. The study of the Connecticut crackdown on speeding, which used an interrupted time series design, would have employed a random assignment rule if the speeding crackdown had been enforced at random from month to month. Under a known assignment rule and multiple replications, the researcher knows the factor responsible for the sequence in which the single unit goes into and out of each condition. In such designs, the known assignment rule can be time, age, or performance level on a test. Finally, under an unknown assignment rule, the order in which the single unit is exposed to the various conditions is determined by unknown factors. This assignment rule is extremely common in interrupted time series designs, such as the Connecticut crackdown study. In that study, the researchers were not aware of all the factors that were responsible for the state's instituting the crackdown when it did.

Relating Research Designs and Validities

Now we can turn our attention to the central topic of this chapter: how research design decisions affect research validity. We will discuss the implications of each of the five research design distinctions for each of the three types of validity.

Internal Validity. Two of the five distinctions among research designs have implications for the researcher's ability to eliminate threats to internal validity: the number of conditions and the type of assignment rule. Recall once again the concern of internal validity: Are differences between conditions due in fact to the conditions themselves, or can other rival hypotheses explain the differences between conditions?

Clearly, a research design must have multiple conditions before the researcher can begin to ask questions about internal validity. Comparisons between conditions are essential in establishing differences. However, while multiple conditions are necessary in a research design for achieving high internal validity, they are certainly not sufficient. Given multiple conditions, what hypothetical result could a research design yield that would indicate perfect internal validity? A research design would be internally valid if there were no differences between conditions when the conditions had no impact at all. In other words, in an internally valid study, if we knew that conditions made no difference, we would find no differences.

The assignment rule used in deciding the condition under which an observation is taken is of fundamental importance for achieving internal validity. On the average, a random assignment rule produces the condition of perfect internal validity. Under a random assignment rule, we do not expect observations in the various conditions to differ on the average in the absence of condition effects. This is true whether units are nested within conditions or crossed with conditions. In the former case, where different units are observed under different conditions, a random assignment rule assures that observations of different units will not differ on the average in the absence of condition differences. In the latter case, when the same units are observed in all conditions, a random assignment rule does the same thing, because it assures that conditions and order of observation of units in those conditions are not confounded on the average.

With a known and nonrandom assignment rule, internal validity can be achieved if two conditions are met. First, the known assignment rule must be statistically controlled when conducting the analysis. Second, the assignment rule must relate linearly to the dependent variable if a linear adjustment procedure, such as analysis of covariance, is used to control for the assignment rule (Judd and Kenny, 1981). The rationale behind these conditions is this: Suppose that we are evaluating day care centers, and we know that age of subjects was used to assign them to different centers. If treatment provided by different centers made no difference, we would expect to find differences on the dependent measures between conditions, unless we first equated subjects on age, that is, on the variable used for assignment. Once the assignment rule has been controlled, then no differences between conditions will be observed on the average in the absence of treatment effects. In order to control adequately for the assignment rule, we need to know the form of its relationship with the dependent variable, that is, whether the relationship is linear, quadratic, or something else.

With an unknown assignment rule, it is very difficult to arrive at bias-free estimates of condition effects. Depending on the assumptions that are made about the nature of the unknown assignment rule and on the pattern of growth over units of time, it is sometimes possible to use pretreatment measures of the outcome variable to control the assignment rule. The assumptions behind such adjustments are quite stringent, however (Judd and Kenny,

1981). With an unknown assignment rule, the internal validity of a study is always in doubt.

In summary, then, both multiple conditions and either a random or a known assignment rule are necessary for a design to have internal validity. When the assignment rule is known, differences between conditions can be calculated only after the assignment rule is adequately controlled. When the assignment rule is unknown, internal validity can rarely, if ever be achieved.

Conclusion Validity. Conclusion validity is concerned with the precision or power of a research design to detect a relationship between independent and dependent variables, should one exist. All the design distinctions that we have made have implications for conclusion validity.

If there is only one condition, a study has no conclusion validity, for the same reason that it has no internal validity. That is, no relationship between the independent and dependent variables can be detected if the condition is not a variable.

When there are multiple conditions, the distinction between units nested within conditions and units crossed with conditions can have a major impact on conclusion validity. When multiple units are observed in each condition, designs in which units are crossed with conditions are generally more powerful than designs in which units are nested within conditions. This is true whenever there are differences among units in their typical response, regardless of the type of assignment rule. Designs in which units are crossed with conditions permit the research to control statistically for unit differences, so long as there are multiple units.

The type of assignment rule used in a research design can also affect conclusion validity. In considering internal validity, we argued that the researcher must control a known assignment rule statistically in order to achieve internal validity. By definition, there is apt to be a high correlation between the assignment rule and the independent variable, since the assignment rule determines condition. When the relationship between the independent and dependent variables is estimated and the assignment variable is controlled, power will decrease to the extent that the independent variable and the assignment variable are correlated. In formal terms, the assignment variable and the independent variables are colinear. Colinearity decreases power. With a known assignment variable, there is a trade-off between internal validity and conclusion validity. To have an internally valid result, the assignment rule needs to be controlled, but controlling it reduces the power of the test of treatment effects. With an unknown assignment rule, this trade-off persists, although it is not as clear. When the assignment rule is unknown, we attempt to increase internal validity by controlling for pretreatment measures of the dependent variable. To the extent that pretreatment measures of the dependent variable and the independent variable are correlated, power is reduced. Here, the trade-off is not as clear as it is when the assignment rule is known, since controlling for the pretreatment responses does not necessarily increase internal validity.

Statistical power increases as the number of observations within conditions increases. Hence, the conclusion validity of a research design tends to increase as both n, the number of units within condition, and r, the number of replications, increase. If there is only one observation per condition ($n = 1$ and $r = 1$), a design has no conclusion validity, since the mean square for error cannot be calculated to test the significance of condition effects. A design in which units are nested within conditions and only a single unit is observed in each condition has very limited conclusion validity, even if there are many replications. In such a case, differences between conditions are differences between units. However, the mean square for error is based on observations from a single unit. Hence, to the extent that such observations are not independent, conclusion validity is reduced.

In summary, design distinctions affect conclusion validity in several ways: A design has no conclusion validity if there is only one condition. When there are multiple conditions, a design has no conclusion validity if there is only one observation per condition. When there are multiple units per condition, designs in which units are crossed with conditions are usually more powerful than designs in which units are nested within conditions. Designs with a random assignment rule tend to be more powerful than designs with other rules. Finally, the greater the number of observations within conditions, the higher the conclusion validity.

Construct Validity. Construct validity refers to the extent that the variables, samples, and settings used in the research are representative of the theoretical constructs, populations, and settings to which we seek to generalize. Construct validity thus defined can be achieved through two procedures. First, the researcher must define with precision the theoretical construct, population, or setting to which generalization is sought. These definitions will give rise to multiple operational definitions or indicators. Second, the researcher should choose multiple, diverse indicators for any construct and operationalize it in the research in multiple ways. To generalize to a population, the researcher should use a representative sample of subjects from that population. To generalize to theoretical constructs or settings, the researcher should choose multiple indicators. While these two procedures for maximizing construct validity can be adopted regardless of the research design employed, they are more easily accomplished in some designs than in others.

The type of assignment rule can have an impact on construct validity. A random assignment rule implies that any observation could potentially be taken under any treatment condition. As a result, it is often necessary to scale down theoretical conditions of interest in order to gain sufficient control to use a random assignment rule. For example, suppose that a researcher is interested in the effects of academic performance upon students' self-esteem. The researcher could be interested in examining the effects of performance over a full year in college. However, if the researcher is committed to use of a random assignment rule, the treatment might have to be scaled down considerably. It is both impractical and unethical to assign students at random to success or failure in academic performance. In essence, then, the commitment to a random assignment rule can force the researcher to trade construct validity for internal validity. In a similar sort of way, a random assignment rule can reduce the construct validity of the sample. That is, in order to use a random assignment rule, the research may have to be conducted in special circumstances requiring the voluntary participation of subjects. However, generalization to a population of interest becomes difficult when the sample selects itself.

We have seen that designs in which units are crossed with conditions tend to have higher conclusion validity than designs in which units are nested within conditions. However, for some types of independent variables, designs in which units are crossed with conditions can have lower construct validity than designs in which units are nested within conditions. For instance, if research seeks to evaluate the effects on degree of prejudice of integrated and segregated living patterns, it is quite unlikely that subjects will be observed in both conditions during the course of the research. If the researcher is adamant about using a design in which subjects are crossed with conditions, it may be necessary to scale down the treatment construct. Instead of looking at residential integration or segregation, it could become necessary to explore interracial contact in short-term social groups. Hence, construct validity would be considerably reduced for the original construct of interest.

Since construct validity requires use of multiple and diverse indicators, variables, and settings, designs in which all observations are taken from a single unit ($n = 1$) necessarily have low construct validity if we wish to generalize to a broader population. Generalizations to a population of interest are clearly hampered when only a single unit from that population is sampled.

The number of replications can also affect construct validity. If data are gathered from every subject repeatedly, we may be able to see how treatments affect responses over time and in different settings. In such cases, multiple replications can increase the construct validity of the research setting.

In summary, the ability to generalize from a research design to theoretical phenomena of interest can be hampered by designs in which a single unit is observed, a random assignment rule is used, subjects are crossed with conditions, or there are no replications.

Conclusion. As we have seen, distinctions among research designs are strongly related to research validity. Any design affects the validity of research. Clearly, no single design or set of designs provides all three validities in equal measure. Rather, there are trade-offs among validities. Designs that are quite useful in some ways can be less adequate in other ways.

Validity Problems Arising from Design Misclassification

Validity problems arise not only from the research design chosen but also from erroneous beliefs about the type of research design under which data have been collected. Problems of internal validity and conclusion validity can arise when analysis of data proceeds as if the data had been collected from one design when in fact some other design was used. Two different types of design misclassification are likely to affect research validity: misclassification due to incorrect definition of the unit of analysis; and misclassification due to incorrect definition of the assignment rule.

Incorrect Definition of the Unit of Analysis. Responses from a single unit are not independent of one another. When the unit of analysis is defined incorrectly, the researcher is likely to ignore dependencies in the data. When such dependencies are ignored, problems of conclusion validity arise.

Two different types of dependencies can be ignored if the researcher defines the unit of analysis incorrectly. First, it is possible that responses in different conditions are not independent of one another. For example, suppose a study is conducted to evaluate two different marital counseling programs. Individuals are assigned to one condition or the other in such a way that they and their spouse are in different conditions. If the individual is used as the unit of analysis, dependencies between conditions due to spouses' similarities will be ignored by the researcher. Because of the dependence between conditions, the researcher should define the couple, rather than the individual, as the unit of analysis. The correct unit of analysis, that is, the couple, is crossed with conditions. If the researcher defines the individual as the unit of analysis, the researcher misclassifies the research design as one in which units are nested within conditions.

The second type of dependence that can be ignored if the unit is incorrectly defined is within condition. Using the preceding example once again, suppose that individuals are assigned to conditions so that they and their spouse are in the same condition. If the individual is used as the unit of analysis, dependencies within condition due to spouses' similarities will be ignored by the researcher. Because of the dependence, the correct unit of analysis is again the couple, and it is observed twice, once for each spouse. In this case, the researcher who defines the unit as the individual confuses replications within a unit with multiple units.

The effects of these two types of dependencies upon conclusion validity depend upon the relationship between responses within couples. For most dependent variables, the response of one spouse is likely to correlate positively with the response of the other spouse. Such positive correlation could be expected, for instance, if the dependent variable were judgments of marital harmony. When dependencies between conditions are ignored because the unit has been incorrectly defined, positively correlated responses are likely to result in Type II statistical errors. It is possible to miss treatment effects when they are in fact there. When dependencies within conditions are ignored because the unit has been incorrectly defined, positively correlated responses are likely to result in Type I statistical errors. Treatment effect may be reported when in fact none exists.

For some dependent variables, the response of one spouse can correlate negatively with the response of the other spouse. Such negative correlation could be expected, for example, if the dependent variable were judgments of the percentage of housework done by each spouse. When dependencies between conditions are ignored, negatively correlated responses are likely to result in Type I statistical errors, with a treatment effect reported when none actually exists. When dependencies within conditions are ignored, negatively correlated responses are likely to result in Type II statistical errors.

Incorrect Definition of the Assignment Rule. Designs can also be misclassified as a result of errors in defining the type of assignment rule. Such misclassifications cause problems of internal validity. Occasionally, researchers presume that a random assignment rule has been employed when in fact one has not. As a result, estimates of the treatment effect are quite likely to be biased. A random assignment rule should be presumed only when it has been guaranteed by use of a table of random numbers or some equivalent procedure.

Fairly frequently, a design with an unknown assignment rule is analyzed as if the rule were known. This happens whenever analysis of covariance is used to adjust for pretreatment differences between treatment conditions. Bias in the estimate of the treatment effect is likely to result unless the pretreatment variables that are controlled constitute the assignment rule.

Conclusion

In this chapter, we have identified four dimensions that discriminate among social research designs in an informative way. We have related these distinctions among designs to research validities and shown the implications of design decisions for the informativeness of research results. Finally, we have identified problems of validity that arise when designs are misclassified.

Throughout, our goal has been to encourage social researchers to identify the strengths and weaknesses of particular designs before they use them. The validities occasionally conflict. Researchers who are aware of the strengths and weaknesses of each type of design and who realize the potential trade-offs among research validities are in a good position to decide which design is best for the problem at hand.

References

Ball, S., and Bogatz, G. A. *The First Year of Sesame Street: An Evaluation.* Princeton: Educational Testing Service, 1970.

Campbell, D. T., and Stanley, J. C. *Experimental and Quasi-Experimental Designs for Research.* Chicago: Rand McNally, 1963.

Cook, T. D., and Campbell, D. T. *Quasi Experimentation: Design Analysis Issues for Field Settings.* Chicago: Rand McNally, 1979.

Cronbach, L. J., and Meehl, P. E. "Construct Validity in Psychological Tests." *Psychological Bulletin,* 1955, *52,* 281–302.

Hardin, E., and Borus, M. E. *The Economic Benefits and Costs of Retraining.* Lexington, Mass.: Heath, 1971.

Judd, C. M., and Kenny, D. A. *Estimating the Effects of Social Interventions.* New York: Cambridge University Press, 1981.

Rees, A. "The Graduated Work Incentive Experiment: An Overview of the Labor Supply Results." *Journal of Human Resources,* 1974, *9,* 158–180.

Ross, H. L., and Campbell, D. T. "The Connecticut Speed Crackdown: A Study of the Effects of Legal Change." In H. L. Ross (Ed.), *Perspectives on the Social Order: Readings in Sociology.* New York: McGraw-Hill, 1968.

Seaver, W. B., and Quarton, R. J. "Social Reinforcement of Excellence: Dean's List and Academic Achievement." Paper presented at the 44th annual meeting of the Eastern Psychological Assocation, Washington, D.C., May 1973.

Thistlethwaite, D. L., and Campbell, D. T. "Regression-Discontinuity Analysis: An Alternative to the Ex Post Facto Experiment." *Journal of Educational Psychology,* 1960, *51,* 309–317.

Charles M. Judd is associate professor in the Department of Psychology at the University of Colorado at Boulder.

David A. Kenny is associate professor in the Department of Psychology at the University of Connecticut.

Why do subjects and researchers disagree
about the how and why of subjects' behavior?

Face Validity from
Multiple Perspectives

Louise ,H. Kidder

As a rule, we do not ask subjects to draw their own conclusions about the effects
of a treatment, the meaning of an action, or the cause of a behavior. Instead,
we as researchers provide feedback to subjects and inform them about the
causes or meanings of their actions. There are instances, however, in which
subjects draw their own conclusions, and these reveal some interesting disagreements between researchers and their subjects. I will examine the sources
of disagreement and discuss why research can seem to be valid from one perspective and invalid from another. I am concerned with disagreements not
only between researchers and their subjects but also between researchers and
the groups from which their subjects are drawn and to which the results will be
generalized. Research results always require interpretation, and different constituencies are likely to make different interpretations.

 The simplest assessment of validity, which uses no statistical techniques, is called *face validity*. When applied as a minimal criterion to research
measures, it is assessed by experts who can look at a measuring instrument

 I wish to thank Richard D. Ashmore, Howard S. Becker, Ronnie Janoff-Bul-
man, David Kipnis, Joseph E. McGrath, Ralph Rosnow, and Carolyn Wood Sherif
for helpful comments on earlier drafts of this chapter.

D. Brinberg, L. Kidder (Eds.). *New Directions for Methodology of Social and Behavioral Science: Forms of Validity
in Research,* no. 12. San Francisco: Jossey-Bass, June 1982.
  41

and say whether it seems like an appropriate measure on its face. If we apply this same minimal criterion to research conclusions, we encounter a new problem — choosing the experts. There are numerous groups of potential experts who can assess the face validity of research results and conclusions, and they are likely to disagree, especially about research that has implications for social policy or action. The potential for disagreement is clearest in applied or evaluation research. Program funders, administrators, recipients, and onlookers often have different criteria for what constitutes success and for identifying the relevant outcomes. Even with basic research, however, there are different parties to the research process, notably the researcher and the subjects, to whom the results are generalized, and they may disagree about the causes, effects, or interpretations of events (Becker, 1967).

Applied to measurement, face validity is a simple criterion, and as a result, it tends to be treated lightly, it is seldom discussed, and it is often dismissed as superficial. Applied to research conclusions, face validity is a more complex issue, resembling construct validity, although it lacks a statistical solution. For instance, two parties who disagree about the "cause" of women's alleged "fear of success" in research like Matina Horner's (Horner, 1968) early studies are disagreeing about what the phenomenon should be called. One may call it an intrapsychic fear or motive to avoid success, while the other may call it a realistic appraisal of what happens when sex-role stereotypes are violated. The former term points to an intrapsychic cause; the latter, to a cultural pattern. Therefore, when different parties assess research conclusions and judge them valid or invalid on their face, they can disagree about the proper name of either the cause or the effect, and in so doing they are assessing the construct validity of a process.

To examine how and why different parties can fail to agree about the face validity of research conclusions, I have identified three points of disagreement. The first point of disagreement is about the causes of behavior. Where we look for causes in the complex set of causal chains depends upon our point of view, and researchers and subjects can differ predictably in where they look for causes. The second point of disagreement is about effects. Which of the many possible effects of a given cause that we select will determine whether we conclude that a given cause produced positive, negative, or null results? The third point of disagreement is about the meanings of events, and this involves simultaneous disputes about causes and effects.

Disagreements About Causes

Researchers and Subjects as Observers and Actors. Some disagreements about causes are predictable. Actors and observers have different perspectives on social interactions, and they differ predictably in where they locate the causes of behavior (Jones and Nisbett, 1972). Research subjects and investigators generally occupy the roles of actors and observers, respectively. Like actors, subjects have access to more information about themselves than the researchers do. Their life histories form the background of their current actions, and changes in environmental conditions stand out in relief against that background. Thus, they attend to the environment, locate causes for their actions outside themselves, and make situational attributions. For researchers, their subjects stand out in relief against a background of situational forces. Consequently, they make causal attributions that locate the sources of behavior in the persons.

In Milgram's (1963) studies of obedience, the subjects and the researchers differed predictably in their attribution of causality and responsibility. The subjects indicated during the debriefing that they held the experimenter responsible for the shocks that they had given. During the experiment, subjects said such things as "You're going to keep giving him, what, 450 volts every time?" They pointed to the experimenter as the cause of the shocks. One subject, worried about the learner's health, repeatedly asked the experimenter, "You accept all responsibility?" From the experimenter's point of view, the subjects were responsible for obeying orders and for inflicting harm on the learner. From the subjects' point of view, the experimenter was responsible, because the experimenter insisted that the subjects inflict harm. In the negotiations that occurred during the debriefing, neither party questioned the joint role of the commands from the experimenter and the obedience from the subjects, but they disagreed over the relative emphasis. Subjects held the experimenter more responsible than themselves and vice versa. Both exhibited a self-serving bias in their attributions (Miller and Ross, 1975), and they made the predictable attributions of actors and observers. As actors, the subjects located the cause of their behavior in the situation, that is, in the experimenter's insistence, and as observers, the experimenters located the cause of the subjects' behavior in them as persons, that is, in human nature. Milgram concludes his film of the obedience studies with the note that "human nature cannot be counted upon" to insulate us from the powers of government to command its citizens to commit acts of violence.*

The subjects in Milgram's experiments disagreed with the researcher not only because they occupied different positions but also because they were deceived on two counts. The subjects were led to believe that the learner was receiving a shock when the subject pressed the lever when in fact no shock was delivered, and they were told that, while the shocks could be painful, they were not dangerous. The filmed account of the experiments shows that sub-

---

*Obedience, copyright 1965 by Stanley Milgram, distributed by the New York University Film Library. Extracts quoted with permission.

jects believed the first allegation — that the learner was receiving a shock — but that they were uncertain about the second. They had conflicting information about the dangers involved. The experimenter said that the shocks could be painful but that they were not dangerous, while the words printed on the shock apparatus said, "Danger . . . Severe Shock . . . XXXX . . . 450 Volts." The subjects' own eyes and ears told them that the shocks were both painful and dangerous, but the experimenter said that there was no danger. Caught between conflicting messages, the subjects negotiated with the experimenter and held him responsible for what happened. They acknowledged that their fingers were on the shock levers and thus that they were a proximal cause of the learner's discomfort, but they located the ultimate cause and therefore the final responsibility with the experimenter (Harvey and Rule, 1978; Kidder and Cohn, 1979).

The causal attributions that experimenters make are not necessarily trait attributions. Most social psychologists, in fact, are probably not trait theorists, for they examine the effects of environmental conditions. Milgram manipulated several environmental conditions and found that subjects disobeyed an authority's commands when they had confederates who also disobeyed and that they administered fewer shocks when they had to force the learner's hand onto the shock plate (Milgram, 1963).

There is often a difference, however, between the external causes that researchers identify and the external causes that subjects identify. For instance, in cognitive dissonance research (Festinger and Carlsmith, 1959), subjects who participated in a dull experiment and then received a small sum of money for telling someone else that the task was really interesting subsequently rated the task as more interesting than subjects who told the same lie for a large sum. The researchers concluded that external circumstances were the cause of the subjects' ratings: The $1 payment was external justification for telling a lie, so subjects sought internal justification and called the task truly interesting. The subjects also concluded that something outside themselves made them call the dull task interesting, but they did not identify the small payment as the cause. They pointed to the stimulus properties of the task; the subjects found redeeming features in an otherwise dull task. Dissonance theorists point to the small payment and the subsequent dissonance arousal as the cause of the subjects' reports. Subjects point to features of the stimulus to explain their reports (Jones and Nisbett, 1972).

Nisbett and Wilson (1977) report a series of studies in which the subjects and the researchers identified different causes for the subjects' behaviors. For instance, researchers asked subjects to select one of four nightgowns and one of four identical pairs of nylon stockings. When subjects were asked why they had selected a particular gown or pair of stockings, they referred to qualities of the gowns or the stockings. The researchers, having alternated the positions of the items, demonstrated that the subjects chose not according to appearance but according to position — the further that an item was to the right, the more frequently that item was selected. The subjects attributed their behavior to properties of the stimulus — that is, to quality or appearance — and the researchers attributed it to external circumstances — that is, to position. No subject noticed a position effect. The researchers concluded that the subjects were wrong and that their verbal reports could not be trusted. I reach a different conclusion. The subjects were fooled into thinking that they could discriminate among four indiscriminably attractive gowns or four identical pairs of stockings. Thus, it was the situation, rather than their verbal reports, that could not be trusted. That rigged situation resembles real-life situations in which consumers are given a choice among essentially identical products, but it is not representative of most choice points in people's lives, where they select stimuli rather than positions. The subjects, therefore, were wrong about the cause of their selection because the situation itself was rigged and unrepresentative.

In the preceding examples, the researchers and their subjects disagree about the causes of the subjects' behavior for two reasons. First, researchers have access to more information and to different information when they deceive their subjects. As a result, they attribute subjects' behavior to causes that the subjects are not always aware of, such as the insufficient justification of a small reward or the position of a product. Second, even in situations where there is no deception, subjects and researchers have access to different information because they occupy different positions as actors and observers. Deception limits the face validity of research because it creates a rigged situation, but even when subjects are not deceived, they are likely to differ from researchers in where they locate causes.

Researchers and Subjects with Different Theories and Ideologies. Some disagreements between researchers and the people whom they study resemble disagreements among researchers. They can hold different ideological and theoretical beliefs. Although we often design research to study the effects of one or two variables, we acknowledge that a complete understanding of the origins of any effect requires that we examine multiple causal chains (Brickman, Ryan, and Wartman, 1975; Kidder and Cohn, 1979). By selecting one of many possible independent variables, we place our emphasis at one point on one of many causal chains. These different causal chains represent complementary rather than competing explanations. For instance, if we study the effect of daytime versus nighttime police patrols on the incidence of crime, we have selected only one of many possible causes of the crime rate. Other causes include the cohesiveness of neighborhoods, levels of unemployment, use of personal and home protection devices, and so on. Each of these factors occupies a position in a separate causal chain.

Although these alternative chains represent complementary rather than competing explanations, they imply different solutions that compete in the political arena for money, time, and effort. For instance, if we study the effects of police patrols on the crime rate and we find that police patrols have an effect, we imply that the appropriate solution is to introduce more police patrols. However, if we study the influence of neighborhood organization or youth employment on the crime rate and we find an effect, we imply that the appropriate solution is to provide more youth employment programs or to promote neighborhood organization (Kidder and Cohn, 1979).

Several black psychologists have made similar points about the white researcher in black society. There are ideological and political differences between researchers who give person-centered explanations of race differences and researchers who give situation-centered explanations of race differences (Clark, 1973; Gordon, 1973; Nobles, 1973). Both as psychologists and as subjects of research, these black psychologists object to the search for inner causes, whether they be genetic or psychological, because such research does not lead to social change. Locating the causes for social problems within individuals permits us to blame victims rather than social conditions. Gordon (1973, p. 94) calls instead for a black psychology that combines analysis and action.

Similarly, feminists call for replacing genetic or intrapsychic explanations of sex differences with sociocultural explanations (Sherif, 1979). In the late 1960s, Horner (1968) postulated a motive to avoid success in women to explain why women did not aspire or achieve as men did. Since then, many women have said that Horner misidentified the cause (Parlee, 1980; Robbins and Robbins, 1973; Sherif, 1979; Unger, 1979; Wallston, 1979). They disagree with Horner's intrapsychic location of the cause in part because it does not fit their own experience (Parlee, 1980) and in part because it is more useful to view intrapsychic variables as symptoms or consequences than as causes. Horner's intrapsychic explanation also creates no force for social change. As Robbins and Robbins (1973, p. 137) have put it, "As long as it is believed that the lack of success of many professional women is primarily due to their psychological disability, expressed as a 'motive to avoid success,' there will be little incentive to redress some of the tangible external barriers — such as admission quotas, slower rates of promotion, and reluctance to grant tenure — which have stood just as surely in the way of professional advancement."

The absence of face validity imputed to Horner's findings led other researchers to improve on Horner's design. Her study confounded the gender of subjects and stimulus persons. Women responded to a female stimulus cue, Ann, who was first in her class in medical school. Men responded to a male stimulus cue, John, who was also first in his class. When women told stories predicting that Ann would subsequently fail or lead an unhappy life alone or commit suicide, Horner concluded that they were projecting their own motives onto Ann and she deduced from this that women have a motive to avoid success. However, another explanation is that Ann's out-of-role behavior, not women's motives, caused them to tell sad stories about Ann. Subsequent researchers disentangled the gender of subjects and stimulus persons and demonstrated that both men and women fear for someone who succeeds in a role traditionally reserved for the opposite sex (Monahan, Kuhn, and Shaver, 1974). The failure of Horner's original interpretation was a failure of face validity. It did not ring true to some women and men, who subsequently developed sociocultural rather than intrapsychic explanations (Sherif, 1979).

The critics of intrapsychic explanations for apparent race and sex differences have called for causal analyses that would lead to social action. Intrapsychic explanations of self-hatred blame black people, and intrapsychic explanations of women's career aspirations blame women. Both deflect attention from social change to personal change. Critics of intrapsychic explanations do not deny that social and cultural conditions can have intrapsychic correlates, but they regard those correlates as consequences, not as causes.

In summary, when the subjects of research disagree with researchers about causes, they may do so for two reasons: First, they occupy different positions, as actors rather than observers, and they have access to different information. Second, they disagree about which of the many contributing causes are the important ones, whose discovery suggests solutions to problems.

Disagreements About Effects

Research conclusions can lack face validity from the perspective of either the subjects or the population to which findings will be generalized if the reported effects of a treatment seem implausible or irrelevant. These differences of opinion can arise from several different sources. First, if the researcher examines manifest functions or public performances, while the subjects focus instead on latent functions or private performances, or vice versa, researcher and subjects are likely to reach different conclusions. Second, as with causes, subjects and researchers have access to different information about effects. The differences arise not from their positions as actors and observers but because they gather different types of information at different times. Finally, subjects and researchers can disagree about the relevance or importance of various effects and use different criteria for what constitutes a successful treatment.

Latent Versus Manifest Functions, Private Versus Public Actions. Reading about gender differences in reward allocations, I found myself objecting to the repeated finding that men allocate rewards in proportion to contribution, while women allocate rewards equally (Leventhal and Lane, 1970). Men who distributed rewards between themselves and a less-deserving partner took more for themselves, following the rule of equity, and women who distributed rewards gave themselves and their partners identical amounts, following the rule of equality. These sex differences were reported repeatedly, with adults, with children, with real partners, and with fictional others. In spite of the repeated evidence, the effect of subjects' gender was not plausible to me because it did not fit either with my personal experience or with my observations as a teacher.

I had students work on group projects and asked them how they wanted to distribute the group grade. I explained that if I gave a grade of B to a group project, the members could divide it equally, so that everyone received a B, or they could divide it proportionally, so that some received A's, some received B's, and some received C's, provided that the group average remained B. The groups always agreed that the grade should be divided equally. However, individual students sometimes came to me in private to protest. They felt that they had contributed more to the project than other students and believed that they deserved an A, while others deserved a C. In private, they proposed an equitable, not an equal, distribution. The students who came to me were always women. They were not, therefore, conforming to the research findings that women prefer equality, while men prefer equity, at least not when they expressed their opinions privately. When I subsequently asked students to let me know in writing, anonymously, but with their gender indicated, how they preferred to allocate awards, I found women choosing equity. That is, they reported having done more of the work, so therefore they deserved more of the reward (Kidder, Bellettirie, and Cohn, 1977).

I then designed an experiment to test the effect of anonymity on reward allocations by men and women to themselves and to a less-deserving partner. In one condition, the subjects believed that their allocations would be public, and in the other condition, they were assured that their decisions would remain private. In the public condition, men chose equity and women chose equality. In private, each did the opposite. The public behavior conformed to the findings of previous literature, but the private choices did not. The apparent sex effects in the earlier literature disappeared in private and were even reversed. The sex effects reported earlier had no face validity for me because they contradicted my personal experience and my observations of the choices that men and women made in private. By making the public-versus-private condition a variable, I uncovered the out-of-role behavior that I had observed informally, and I found different sex effects.

Research that uncovers effects can have face validity for some people but not for others. Nancy Henley's research on the functions of touch uncovers some latent functions which contradict the cover story that touching is a sign of affection (Henley, 1977; Parlee, 1980). Henley's work identifies instances "when the act of touching has a different meaning: When touching is asymmetrical . . . the act of touching represents a statement or affirmation of power differences" (Parlee, 1980, pp. 1–2). By observing the conditions under which one person touches another and that touch is not reciprocated, Henley noted that touching can serve to bestow low status rather than to convey affection. These two effects of touch — bestowing low status and conveying affection — occur in different contexts, and they have different causes. Identification of effects, therefore, is not always separable from identification of causes, particularly when the two involve people's intentions. Disagreements over such effects are disagreements about the meanings of events, and as such they are questions about construct validity.

Just as causal attributions sometimes contain a self-serving bias, interpretations of effects can serve the purposes of actors or observers (Miller and Ross, 1975). Some people may choose to believe that asymmetrical touching affirms affection rather than power. There is no research on how actors and observers or how doers and those who are "done unto" perceive effects. Consciousness-raising movements among low-status groups (black people, women, the physically disabled) suggest that low-status persons do not automatically perceive asymmetrical acts as affirmations of power differences but that they learn to assign such meaning to asymmetrical touch or to other behavior.

Availability of Information About Effects. The timing of the research process makes it almost inevitable that researchers will have more of one kind of information about the effects of a treatment than will their subjects. Individual subjects can assess the effects of a treatment upon themselves immediately. The researcher can assess the effects upon a large group of subjects, but only after all have participated. Even in research that provides for full and accurate debriefing, subjects cannot know what the overall effects of a treatment are until long after they have participated. Thus, if a researcher asks subjects to assess the effects of a treatment, they cannot make a fully informed judgment, because all the data are not available.

This inevitable difference between what subjects know when they participate and what a researcher knows at the end of a study accounts for some reported discrepancies between researchers' and subjects' descriptions of effects. The most dramatic discrepancy appeared in the evaluation of a delinquency prevention program, known as the Cambridge-Somerville experiment, begun in 1939 and evaluated thirty years later (McCord, 1978). Boys between the ages of five and thirteen were randomly assigned to a delinquency prevention treatment group or to a control group. Boys in the treatment group received scholastic tutoring, medical and psychiatric attention, opportunities to attend summer camp, access to youth activities, and biweekly visits from social workers. Boys in the control group received no special services. The treatment lasted five years.

In a thirty-year follow-up of men who had been in the treatment and control groups, McCord found that men in the treatment group fared worse on every measure where there was a significant difference. Equal numbers of men in the treatment and control groups had been convicted of committing a crime, but of those men, a higher proportion of men in the treatment group had committed more than one crime. Men in the treatment group showed a higher incidence of self-reported alcoholism, ulcers, asthma, and high blood pressure. Equal numbers of men in the treatment and control groups had died by the time of the follow-up, but men in the treatment group had died at an earlier age. Of those who were living, men in the treatment group had lower occupational status on the average than men in the control group. The treatment, therefore, had uniformly negative effects.

There was one exception to this otherwise negative picture. When asked what they thought about the program, two-thirds of the men in the treatment group said that it had been helpful. They said such things as "It helped prepare me for manhood," it gave "better insight on life in general," and it helped them to have "faith and trust in other people" (McCord, 1978, p. 287). According to the subjects' assessment, the treatment helped. By every objective standard, it hurt. Why do they disagree?

The researcher had a better vantage point from which to assess the multiple effects of the treatment and access to longitudinal and cross-sectional archival data. If the subjects had been informed about the higher criminal arrest rate, the alcoholism rates, the lower occupational standing, and the earlier deaths of men in the treatment group, they, too, would probably have concluded that the program had hurt more than it had helped. For this reason, rather than ask who is right, I will examine what the subjects could have meant when they said that the program had helped. Their positive assessment resembles the almost universal finding of evaluations of compensatory education programs: "Regardless of the type of program, duration, or actual results, parents are enthusiastic" (McDill, McDill, and Sprehe, 1969, pp. 43–44).

It is possible that men in the Cambridge-Somerville experiment and parents of children in compensatory education programs are enthusiastic about the fact that they have been offered services that they normally would not receive. They may be responding more to the process than to the outcome (Kidder, 1981a). Perhaps it is the process that they appreciate. Men in the Cambridge-Somerville experiment would not have had access to the summer programs, counseling, or youth activities if they had not been in the treatment group. Without compensatory education programs, participating parents would not have access to organized preschool care for their children. Thus, they may be enthusiastic about the programs not because the programs produce the intended effects but because they provide goods and services that participants would not have had otherwise.

We can imagine similarly discrepant evaluations by researchers and participants in other social programs, such as the negative income tax experiments. Researchers have studied the effect of the program on the number of hours worked. The program is considered a success if recipients of negative income tax benefits do not work less than they have before. I have found no reports of what the recipients had to say about the programs, but I can extrapolate from discrepancies found in evaluations of various negative income tax experiments. The program appears to have different effects on salaried workers and on nonsalaried self-employed farmers (U.S. Department of Health, Education and Welfare, 1978).

Salaried workers are more likely to reduce the number of hours worked than nonsalaried farmers are, particularly in those conditions of the experiment where participants lose their negative income tax benefits at a high rate as they earn increased amounts of money. In some programs, recipients lost as much as 70 percent of their benefits when their salaries rose above a minimum level. In effect, they were taxed on their benefits as if they were in a 70 percent tax bracket. Therefore, they had little incentive to increase the hours worked, because they rapidly lost their benefits. For nonsalaried self-employed farmers, however, the extra hours worked did not produce an immediate increase in their personal earnings. By investing time and labor on their farms, they could eventually realize higher earnings, but these would be delayed, and the workers suffered no loss in their immediate negative income tax benefits. Therefore, self-employed farmers increased the number of hours they worked, and salaried workers decreased the number of hours worked. The same treatment had different effects.

By one criterion, the number of hours worked, the program succeeded among farmers and failed among salaried workers. It is possible, however, that by another criterion, the program succeeded among both groups. What might that other criterion be? If we examine the behaviors of both groups, it appears that both groups tried to maximize the financial returns on their work. For the salaried workers, there was a point of diminishing returns. At that point, they decreased their hours worked, possibly in exchange for more leisure time or for unreported work. For the nonsalaried farmers, there was no immediate point of diminishing returns as long as they could defer their earnings. The goal for both groups appeared to be maximizing returns, not the number of hours worked. Asked to evaluate the negative income tax experiments, both groups could have called it successful by their own criteria. Thus, it is possible for researchers and their subjects to have access to different information, adopt different criteria for success, and attach different meanings to the resulting "effects."

Disagreements About Meanings of Events

The face validity of conclusions rests on the construct validity of measures of both causes and effects. If researchers and subjects disagree about the effects of a treatment like the negative income tax, they are disagreeing about what working means. For a salaried employee, working more means receiving fewer benefits and realizing a small return. For a nonsalaried farmer, working more means receiving the same benefits and realizing a delayed return on the work. For a researcher, working more is better than working less, and presumably it means the same in all instances if that is the criterion used to evaluate the negative income tax experiments. Therefore, researchers and subjects could disagree about the success of the taxation, because they disagree about whether working more is good or bad.

This example illustrates another point: When people disagree about the effects of an experiment, they may also be disagreeing about the causes. For instance, one interpretation of the failure of negative income tax experiments is that the payments produced a disincentive for work. A different interpretation is that the high taxation made it less worthwhile to work. Was it the payment of benefits or the loss of those benefits that made some people work less? When recipients earned money and their income rose above a baseline, they lost their negative income payments at a specified taxation rate. If the rate was 70 percent, they received only 30¢ for every dollar earned above the baseline income level, because their benefits were reduced at the rate of 70¢ for every dollar earned above the baseline. Therefore, in identifying the effects of the experiment, we are also identifying the cause, and in the present instance, the cause could be either payment of benefits or loss of benefits.

The subjects in Milgram's obedience studies who disagreed with Milgram about the meanings of their actions disagreed simultaneously about both causes and effects. Milgram's data have generally been interpreted as showing that subjects obeyed rather than defied the commands. The subjects, however — even those who pressed the maximum-shock lever — described themselves as defying rather than obeying authority. The filmed record of the experiments contains exchanges like the following, which occurred in a debriefing session:

Milgram: The purpose of the experiment was to see how you would react to Mr. Williams' [the experimenter's] authority — whether you would obey it or defy it.

Subject: I defied it! I mean, who the hell is he?

The subject believed he had defied authority because he had not willingly complied but had been coerced. Milgram, however, portrayed this subject as obedient. Another debriefing session contains the following exchange:

Subject: He [the experimenter] kept throwing him [the learner] 450 volts.

Milgram: Who actually pressed the switch?
Subject: I was, but he kept insisting.
Milgram: Why didn't you stop?
Subject: I *did* stop, but he kept telling me to go on.

In such cases, Milgram concluded that the subjects obeyed authority and did not stop, and the subjects concluded that they had defied authority or had stopped.

Rather than trying to determine who is right, I have chosen to examine why the subjects and the researcher disagreed. In the exchanges presented here, they disagree about the effects of commands from authority in part because they disagree about the causes of the subjects' behavior. The subjects said that they defied authority and stopped even when they had pressed the maximum-shock lever. They considered themselves defiant, because at some point they switched responsibility for the shocks from themselves to the experimenter. In one sequence of the film, a subject and the experimenter negotiate responsibility as follows:

Subject: The guy's hollering in there.
Experimenter: Continue, please, go on.
Subject: The guy has a heart condition in there. You want me to go on? He can't stand it. What if something happens to him?
Experimenter: The experiment requires that you continue.
Subject: I refuse to take the responsibility. Who's going to take the responsibility if something happens to that gentleman?
Experimenter: I'm responsible. Continue, please.
Subject: [After a few more shocks] Oh, no. No, I'm not going to kill that man.
Experimenter: The experiment requires that you continue.
Subject: We can't go on if the learner doesn't answer.
Experimenter: If the learner doesn't answer, go on.
Subject: Can't you check in and see if he's alright, please? [to the learner:] Answer, please. Are you alright in there? [to the experimenter:] Something's happened to that man in there. You accept all responsibility?
Experimenter: The responsiblity's mine, correct. Please go on.
Subject: You're going to keep giving him, what, 450 volts every time?

Later, during the debriefing, the subject said to Milgram, "He [the experimenter] kept throwing him 450 volts." The subject had negotiated the responsibility with the experimenter and concluded that it was the experimenter, not himself, who inflicted the shocks on the learner. The subject's interpretation of both the causes of his behavior and the effects of commands from authority differed from Milgram's interpretation. The subject felt that he had stopped and that it was the experimenter who had continued; the subject felt that he had defied authority, not obeyed it.

Drawing Conclusions with Face Validity from Multiple Perspectives

Having identified conclusions that lack face validity from the perspective of a given constituency, I felt obliged to say whether or how we can do research that appears valid from multiple points of view. The question partially provides its own answer. We can conduct research that has validity from more than one constituent's point of view by asking questions and eliciting information from multiple perspectives. For instance, to evaluate the effects of a social program like compensatory education, we can use multiple criteria derived from the points of view of parents, children, teachers, and program administrators. Some criteria may have zero or even negative correlations with one another, because they represent divergent rather than convergent perspectives. The more applied and the more politically sensitive that a research topic is, the greater the potential for disagreement about causes and effects, which makes it all the more urgent that we elicit multiple perspectives. Research on intergroup conflict provides a useful paradigm. The rival groups of Rattlers and Eagles in the Robbers' Cave experiments had different perspectives on who was to blame for the rivalry. Neither group had an exclusive hold on the truth; both holds were necessary to understand the sequence of events (Sherif, 1976; Sherif and others, 1961).

Hastorf and Cantril's (1954) analysis of Dartmouth and Princeton students' perspectives on a hotly contested football game shows that the rivals disagreed not only in their descriptions of how "rough and dirty" the game was but also in their count of how many rules were broken by each team. "The 'game' actually was many different games . . . each version of the events that transpired was just as 'real' to a particular person as other versions were to other people" (Hastorf and Cantril, 1954, p. 132). Therefore, one solution to the problem of maximizing face validity for multiple constituencies is to include more than one perspective in the inquiry. Using the intergroup conflict paradigm, we can take our inquiry a step further and ask how the divergent perspectives developed and how they relate to the circumstances of the relationship (Carolyn Sherif, personal communication).

A second answer to the question of how to do research that has face validity from other people's perspectives is contained in Herbert Blumer's description of how to "catch the process of interpretation through which they construct their actions" (Blumer, 1962, p. 62). He says that "to catch the process, the student must take the role of the acting unit." The presume danger of taking the role of the acting unit is that the researcher may lose his or her objectivity. Blumer counters this by saying that the failure to take the subject's point of view can lead to errors: "To try to catch the interpretive process by remaining aloof as a so-called 'objective' observer and refusing to take the role of the acting unit is to risk the worst kind of subjectivism — the objective observer is likely to fill in the process of interpretation with his own surmises in place of catching the process as it occurs in the experience of the acting unit which uses it" (Blumer, 1962, p. 62). Misplaced objectivity, therefore, can be a source of disagreement between subjects and researchers, because it forces researchers to guess about subjects' interpretations. Participant observation provides a means for researchers to learn what the subjects' interpretations are and reduces the need for guessing.

Participant observation is often suspect because it seems overly subjective. I have shown elsewhere (Kidder, 1981a) that, although participant observation appears to be subjective, it has much in common with quasi-experimental research. Participant observers can make causal analyses and rule out threats to internal validity in much the same way as quasi experimenters. By gathering data over an extended time, a participant observer can develop a time series design, and by gathering longitudinal data on multiple groups, individuals, or institutions, a participant observer can develop multiple time series. The long series of observations enables the participant observer to test rival explanations and to rule out threats to internal validity like a quasi experimenter. The subjective quality of participant observation, therefore, does not preclude causal analysis.

As a rule, participant observers do not use the objective language of independent and dependent variables, but that objective language can disguise rather than eliminate bias. As Carolyn Sherif (1979) points out, intrapsychic explanations for sex differences have been perpetuated by research that appears to be "objective." She adds that, by "glorifying the experiment," we imply that "knowledge is to be gained by studying parts, elements, or variables," and as a result, "much of what goes on is simply ignored" (Sherif, 1979, p. 102). An experiment is no less an interpersonal event than participant observation is, and the artifacts arising from demand characteristics and other unintended features have been amply documented (Rosenthal and Rosnow, 1969). Participant observation is not a panacea, but it can increase the face validity of research, because it enables a researcher to catch the process from a subject's point of view.

Conclusion

Social science research that has face validity need not be like Heider's (1958) naive psychology of personal theories. To do research that has face validity does not require that we accept at face value the theories of naive observers but rather that we include the perspectives of our subjects and other constituencies in our assessment of the causes, effects, and meanings of events. Research with face validity produces a "click of recognition" and a "yes, of course," instead of "yes, but," experience (Parlee, 1980). To develop conclusions with face validity, we do not need to rule out surprises and discoveries. As social scientists, we may never discover something that no one else has known, but we are in a position to discover what many different people know and thereby to learn more than any one person has known before (Howard Becker, personal communication).

References

Becker, H. S. "Whose Side Are We On?" *Journal of Social Problems,* 1967, *14,* 239–247.

Blumer, H. "Society as Symbolic Interaction." In A. Rose (Ed.), *Human Behavior and Social Processes: An Interactionist Approach.* Boston: Houghton Mifflin, 1962.

Brickman, P., Ryan, K., and Wortman, C. B. "Causal Chains: Attribution of Responsibility as a Function of Immediate and Prior Causes." *Journal of Personality and Social Psychology,* 1975, *32,* 1060–1067.

Clark, C. X. "The Role of the White Researcher in Black Society: A Futuristic Look." *Journal of Social Issues,* 1973, *29* (1), 109–118.

Festinger, L., and Carlsmith, T. M. "Cognitive Consequences of Forced Compliance." *Journal of Abnormal and Social Psychology,* 1959, *58,* 203–210.

Gordon, T. "Notes on White and Black Psychology." *Journal of Social Issues,* 1973, *29* (1), 87–96.

Harvey, M. D., and Rule, B. G. "Moral Evaluations and Judgments of Responsibility." *Personality and Social Psychology Bulletin,* 1978, *4* (4), 583–588.

Hastorf, A. H., and Cantril, H. "They Saw a Game: A Case Study." *Journal of Abnormal and Social Psychology,* 1954, *49,* 129–134.

Heider, F. *The Psychology of Interpersonal Relations.* New York: Wiley, 1958.

Henley, N. M. *Body Politics: Power, Sex, and Nonverbal Communication.* Englewood Cliffs, N.J.: Prentice-Hall, 1977.

Horner, M. "Sex Differences in Achievement Motivation and Performance in Competitive and Noncompetitive Situations." Unpublished doctoral dissertation, University of Michigan, 1968.

Jones, E. E., and Nisbett, R E. "The Actor and the Observer: Divergent Perceptions of the Causes of Behavior." In E. E. Jones and others (Eds.), *Attribution: Perceiving the Causes of Behavior.* Morristown, N.J.: General Learning Press, 1972.

Kidder, L. H. "Qualitative Research and Quasi-Experimental Frameworks." In M. B. Brewer and B. E. Collins (Eds.), *Scientific Inquiry and the Social Sciences.* San Francisco: Jossey-Bass, 1981a.

Kidder, L. H. *"Sellitz, Wrightsman, and Cook's Research Methods in Social Relations.* New York: Holt, Rinehart and Winston, 1981b.

Kidder, L. H., Bellettirie, G., and Cohn, E. S. "Secret Ambitions and Public Performances: The Effects of Anonymity on Reward Allocations Made by Men and Women." *Journal of Experimental Social Psychology,* 1977, *13,* 70-80.

Kidder, L. H., and Cohn, E. S. "Public Views of Crime and Crime Prevention." In I. H. Frieze, D. Bar-Tal, and J. S. Carroll (Eds.), *New Approaches to Social Problems: Aplications of Attribution Theory.* San Francisco: Jossey-Bass, 1979.

Leventhal, G. S., and Lane, D. W. "Sex, Age, and Equity Behavior." *Journal of Personality and Social Psychology,* 1970, *15,* 312-316.

McCord, J. "A Thirty-Year Follow-up of Treatment Effects." *American Psychologist,* 1978, *33,* 284-289.

McDill, E. L., McDill, M. S., and Sprehe, J. T. *Strategies for Success in Compensatory Education: An Appraisal of Evaluation Research.* Baltimore, Md.: Johns Hopkins University Press, 1969.

Milgram, S. "Behavioral Study of Obedience." *Journal of Abnormal and Social Psychology,* 1963, *67,* 371-378.

Miller, D. T., and Ross, M. "Self-Serving Biases in the Attribution of Causality: Fact or Fiction?" *Psychological Bulletin,* 1975, *82,* 213-225.

Monahan, L., Kuhn, D., and Shaver, P. "Intrapsychic Versus Cultural Explanations of the 'Fear of Success' Motive." *Journal of Personality and Social Psychology,* 1974, *29* (1), 60-64.

Nisbett, R. E., and Wilson, T. D. "Telling More Than We Know: Verbal Reports on Mental Processes." *Psychological Review,* 1977, *84* (3), 231-259.

Nobles, W. W. "Psychological Research and the Black Self-Concept: A Critical Review." *Journal of Social Issues,* 1973, *29* (1), 11-32.

Parlee, M. B. "Developing Feminist Psychology." Paper presented at the 88th annual meeting of the American Psychological Association, Montreal, 1980.

Robbins, L., and Robbins, E. "Comment on 'Toward an Understanding of Achievement-Related Conflicts in Women'." *Journal of Social Issues,* 1973, *29* (1), 133-137.

Rosenthal, R., and Rosnow, R. (Eds.). *Artifact in Behavioral Research.* New York: Academic Press, 1969.

Sherif, C. W. *Orientation in Social Psychology.* New York: Harper & Row, 1976.

Sherif, C. W. "Bias in Psychology." In J. A. Sherman and E. T. Beck (Eds.), *The Prism of Sex.* Madison: University of Wisconsin Press, 1979.

Sherif, M., Harvey, O. J., White, B. J., Hood, W. R., and Sherif, C. W. *Intergroup Conflict and Cooperation: The Robbers' Cave Experiment.* Normal, Okla.: Institute of Group Relations, 1961.

Unger, R. K. *Female and Male: Psychological Perspectives.* New York: Harper & Row, 1979.

U.S. Department of Health, Education, and Welfare. "The Rural Income Maintenance Experiment." In T. D. Cook and others (Eds.), *Evaluation Studies Review Annual.* Vol. 3. Beverly Hills, Calif.: Sage, 1978.

Wallston, B. S. "What Are the Questions in Psychology of Women? A Feminist Approach to Research." Presidential address for Division 35, American Psychological Association, New York City, 1979.

Louise H. Kidder is associate professor in the Department of Psychology at Temple University.

Quantitative procedures can be used to compare and combine findings from two or more independent studies.

Valid Interpretation of Quantitative Research Results

Robert Rosenthal

The purpose of this chapter is to raise some questions and to describe some procedures that can be useful in the assessment of quantitative results of research. Its focus is on studies that have already met the criteria for achieving reasonable levels of several types of validity. It will be assumed, for example, that the independent and dependent variables have achieved adequate levels of measurement validity (for example, predictive, concurrent, postdictive, convergent, discriminant, content, and construct). It will also be assumed that the research design permits a high degree of internal validity; for example, as in a study that employs random assignment of units to treatments. Finally, it will be assumed that appropriate statistical procedures have been employed, so that, for example, any violations of assumptions underlying the use of such statistics as t, F, and χ^2 are not sufficiently great to alter materially the distribution of the statistic computed from the distribution as it has been tabled.

If so many types of validity are granted to the studies considered in this discussion, what invalidity could be left? External invalidity, of course, and inferential invalidities (that is, type I and type II errors). External validity will

Preparation of this chapter was supported in part by the National Science Foundation.

D. Brinberg, L. Kidder (Eds.). *New Directions for Methodology of Social and Behavioral Science: Forms of Validity in Research*, no. 12. San Francisco: Jossey-Bass, June 1982.

be discussed when we take up the comparison and combination of two or more studies. Inferential invalidities, that is, inferring a zero relationship to be non-zero or inferring a nonzero relationship to be zero, can still occur both at the level of a single study and at the level of a set of studies.

The Single Study

What shall we mean by the *results* of a single study? We shall not mean the conclusion drawn by the investigator, since that is often only vaguely related to the actual results. The metamorphosis that sometimes occurs between the results section and the discussion section is a topic worthy of detailed consideration. For now, it will be enough to note that a fairly ambiguous result often becomes quite smoothed and rounded in the discussion section, so that readers who dwell too little on the results and too much on the discussion can be quite misled as to what actually was found.

We shall also not mean the result of an omnibus F test with $df > 1$ in the numerator or an omnibus χ^2 test with $df > 1$. In both cases, we get answers to questions that are often, perhaps usually, hopelessly imprecise. Only rarely are we really interested in knowing for any fixed-factor analysis of variance or covariance that somewhere in the thicket of df there lurk one or more meaningful answers to meaningful questions that we did not have the foresight to ask of our data. Similarly, there are few occasions when what we really want to know is that somewhere in a contingency table, there is an obtained frequency or two that have strayed too far from the frequency expected for that cell under the null hypothesis.

What we shall mean by the results is the answer to the question: What is the relationship between some variable X and some variable Y? The answer to this question, however, must come in two parts. The first part is an estimate of the magnitude of the relationship, the effect size. The second part is an indication of the accuracy of the estimated effect size, as in a confidence interval placed around the estimate. An alternative to the second part of the answer, not intrinsically more useful but consistent with the existing practices of behavioral researchers, is a test of the significance of the difference between the obtained effect size and the effect size that can be expected under the null hypothesis of no relationship between variables X and Y.

Since the argument has been made that the results of a study with respect to any given relationship can be expressed as an estimate of an effect size plus a test of significance, we would make the relationship between these two quantities explicit. The general relationship is:

$$\text{Test of Significance} = \text{Effect Size} \times \text{Size of Study}.$$

One example of this general relationship is:

$$\chi^2(1) = \phi^2 \times N \tag{1}$$

That is, χ^2 on $df = 1$ is the product of the size of the effect expressed by the product-moment correlation squared multiplied by N, the number of sampling units. Other examples illustrating the general relationship between tests of significance and effect size estimates include:

$$Z = \phi \times \sqrt{N} \tag{2}$$

$$t = (M_1 - M_2)/S \times \sqrt{\frac{n_1 n_2}{n_1 + n_2}} \tag{3}$$

$$F(1, -) = [(M_1 - M_2)/S]^2 \times \frac{n_1 n_2}{n_1 + n_2} \tag{4}$$

Equation 2 shows that the standard normal deviate Z (that is, the square root of χ^2 on 1 df) is the product of the product-moment correlation and the square root of N. Equation 3 shows that t is the product of the effect size ($M_1 - M_2$)/S—sometimes called d, defined as the difference between the means divided by the square root of the pooled variance—and an index of the size of the study that takes account of unequal sample sizes (Cohen, 1977; Glass, 1980). If the sample sizes of the two groups were equal, this second term would simplify to $\sqrt{n/2}$. Equation 4 shows that F with one df in the numerator is the product of the squared ingredients of the right-hand side of equation 3. This is just as it should be, of course, given that $t^2 = F$ when $df = 1$ in the numerator.

In interpreting the results of any study, it is always essential to compute and report some estimate of the effect size. Cohen (1977) has a detailed discussion of a variety of such effect-size estimates, of which the most generally useful appear to be those based on product-moment correlations and those based on standardized differences between the means.

The product-moment correlations are widely used, easily computed from test statistics, and very general in applicability. Thus, product-moment correlations can be used when both variables are continuous (Pearson r), when both variables are in ranked form (Spearman rho), when both variables are dichotomous (phi or ϕ), or when one variable is continuous and one variable is dichotomous (point-biserial r). Product-moment correlations can be computed from $\chi^2(1)$, t, and $F(1, -)$ very readily from the following formulas (Friedman, 1968):

$$\phi = \sqrt{\frac{\chi^2(1)}{N}} \tag{5}$$

$$r = \sqrt{\frac{t^2}{t^2 + df}} \tag{6}$$

$$r = \sqrt{\frac{F(1, -)}{F(1 -) + df \text{ error}}} \tag{7}$$

One problem with the interpretation of r stems from our inclination to square r and then to misinterpret the practical importance associated with any given r. In the final section of this chapter, a method for the display and interpretation of r is presented that seems to be substantially more intuitive and informative than most of our current procedures for reporting effect sizes (Rosenthal and Rubin, in press b).

Standardized differences between the means represent an alternative metric for reporting effect sizes. The difference between the means of two groups is divided either by the square root of the mean square for error or by the standard deviation (that is, by σ rather than S) common to the two treatment conditions. The complex issues governing the choice of the standardizing denominator and complications arising from the use of repeated-measures designs have led me to lean more to the use of r as the effect-size estimate in my most recent work. In most cases (for example, for between-subjects designs, but not necessarily for within-subjects designs), r is very easily derived from d by a formula given by Cohen (1977):

$$r = \frac{d}{\sqrt{d^2 + 4}} \tag{8}$$

Similarly, given r, we can easily obtain d by

$$d = \frac{2r}{\sqrt{1 - r^2}} \tag{9}$$

If the reported results of a study always include both an estimate of effect size and a test of significance (or a related procedure, such as a confidence interval), we can better protect ourselves against the inferential invalidity of type I and type II errors, as we shall see. There is little doubt that, in the social and behavioral sciences, type II errors are far more likely than type I errors (Cohen, 1962, 1977). The frequency of type II errors can be reduced drastically if we attend to the magnitude of the estimated effect size. If we regard an estimate as large and we find a nonsignificant result, it is advisable to decide that variables X and Y are not related. Only if the pooled results of a good many replications point to a very small effect size on the average and if a combined test of significance does not reach our favorite alpha level are we justified in concluding that there is no nontrivial relationship between X and Y. Table 1 summarizes inferential errors and some possible consequences as a joint function of the results of significance testing and the population-effect size.

Two Studies

There appear to be no social or behavioral researchers who are against replication. Yet, despite our very favorable evaluation of the enterprise of replication, there is little evidence that we are very good at making sense of the joint meaning of the results of two or more studies. Happily, this is beginning to change, and there is growing interest in summarizing domains of research (Glass, 1980; Hall, 1980; Pillemer and Light, 1980; Rosenthal, 1978, 1980; Rosenthal and Rubin, 1978, 1980; Smith, 1980).

Even when we are quite rigorous and sophisticated in interpreting the results of a single study, we are often prone to err when interpreting the results of two or more studies. For example, Smith can report a significant relationship between X and Y, only to have Jones publish a rebuttal claiming that there is no such relationship. A closer look at the results of both could show the following:

Smith's study: $t(78) = 2.21$, $p < .05$, $d = .50$, $r = .24$ (see equation 6)

Jones's study: $t(18) = 1.06$, $p > .30$, $d = .50$, $r = .24$ (see equation 6)

Table 1. Combinations of Population-Effect Sizes and Results of Significance Testing as Determinants of Inferential Errors

	Results of Significance Testing	
Population Effect Size	*Not Significant*	*Significant*
Zero	No error	Type I error
Small	Type II error[a]	No error[c]
Large	Type II error[b]	No error

[a]Low power may lead to failure to detect the true effect but if the true effect is quite small the costs of this error may not be too great.
[b]Low power may lead to failure to detect the true effect and with a substantial true effect the costs of this error may be very great.
[c]Although not an inferential error, if the effect size is *very* small and N is very large we may mistake a result that is merely very significant for one that is of practical importance.

Smith's results are more significant than Jones's, to be sure, but the studies are in perfect agreement on their estimated sizes of effect, as defined by either d or r. Further, comparison of the respective significance levels reveals that these ps are not significantly different ($p = .42$; the details of the computation are given in the next paragraph). Clearly, Jones was wrong in claiming that he had failed to replicate Smith's results. Thus, we shall begin by considering some procedures for comparing quantitatively the results of two independent studies, such as studies conducted with different research participants.

Comparing Studies

Significance Testing. Ordinarily, when we compare the results of two studies, we are more interested in comparing their effect sizes than their p values. However, sometimes we cannot do any better than to compare their p values, and this is how we do it (Rosenthal and Rubin, 1979a): For each of the two test statistics, we obtain an accurate p level. That is, if $t(30) = 3.03$, we give p as .0025, not as $< .05$. Extended tables of the t distribution are helpful here (Federighi, 1959). For each p, we find Z, the standard normal deviate corresponding to the p value. Both ps should be one-tailed. The corresponding Zs will have the same sign if both studies show effects in the same direction, and they will have different signs if the results show effects in opposite directions. The difference between the two Zs, when divided by $\sqrt{2}$, yields a new Z that corresponds to the p value that the difference between the Zs could be as large or larger if the two Zs did not really differ.

Recapitulating,

$$\frac{Z_1 - Z_2}{\sqrt{2}} \text{ is distributed as } Z. \tag{10}$$

Example 1. Studies A and B yield results in opposite directions, and neither is significant. One p is .06, one-tailed, while the other p is .12, one-tailed but in the opposite direction. The Zs corresponding to these ps are found in a table of the normal curve to be $+1.56$ and -1.18. (Note that the opposite signs indicate results in opposite directions.) Using equation 10, we obtain

$$\frac{Z_1 - Z_2}{\sqrt{2}} = \frac{(1.56) - (-1.18)}{1.41} = 1.94$$

as the Z of the difference between the two p values or their corresponding Zs. The p value associated with a Z of 1.94 is .026 one-tailed, or .052 two-tailed.

Thus, the two p values differ significantly, which suggests that we can draw different inferences from the different p values of these two studies.

Example 2. Studies A and B yield results in the same direction, and both are significant. One p is .04, the other is .000025. The Zs corresponding to these ps are 1.75 and 4.06. (Since both Zs are in the same tail, they have the same sign.) From equation 10, we obtain

$$\frac{Z_1 - Z_2}{\sqrt{2}} = \frac{(4.06) - (1.75)}{1.41} = 1.64$$

as the Z of the difference. The p associated with that Z is .050 one-tailed, or .100 two-tailed. As a result, we may want to conclude that the two p values differ significantly.

Example 3. Studies A and B yield results in the same direction, but one is significant ($p = .05$), while the other is not ($p = .06$). This example illustrates the worst-case scenario for inferential errors, where investigators conclude that the two results are inconsistent because one is significant and the other is not. Regrettably, this example is not merely hypothetical: Just such errors have been made and documented (Rosenthal and Gaito, 1963, 1964). The Zs corresponding to these ps are 1.64 and 1.55. From equation 10, we obtain,

$$\frac{Z_1 - Z_2}{\sqrt{2}} = \frac{(1.64) - (1.55)}{1.41} = .06$$

as the Z of the difference between a p value of .05 and a p value of .06. The p value associated with this difference is .476 one-tailed, or .952 two-tailed. This example shows clearly just how nonsignificant the difference between significant and nonsignificant results can be.

Effect-Size Estimation. When we ask whether two studies are telling the same story, what we are usually asking is: Are the results, in terms of the estimated effect size, reasonably consistent with each other, or are they significantly inconsistent? For the purpose of the present chapter, the discussion will be restricted to r as the effect-size indicator, but analogous procedures are available for comparing such other effect-size indicators as Cohen's (1977) d or differences between proportions (Hsu, 1980; Rosenthal and Rubin, in press a).

For each of the two studies to be compared, we compute the effect size r, and for each of these rs, we find the associated Fisher z, which is defined as $\frac{1}{2} \log_e[(1 + r)/(1 - r)]$. Tables to convert our obtained rs to Fisher zs are available in most introductory textbooks on statistics. Then, when N_1 and N_2 represent the number of sampling units (for example, of subjects) in each of our two studies, the quantity

$$\frac{z_1 - z_2}{\sqrt{\dfrac{1}{N_1 - 3} + \dfrac{1}{N_2 - 3}}} \text{ is distributed as } Z \qquad (11)$$

Example 4. Studies A and B yield results in opposite directions, with effect sizes of $r = .60$ (N = 15) and $r = -.20$ (N = 100), respectively. The Fisher zs corresponding to these rs are .69 and $-.20$, respectively. (Note that the opposite signs of the zs correspond to the opposite signs of the rs.) Then, from equation 11, we obtain

$$\frac{z_1 - z_2}{\sqrt{\dfrac{1}{N_1 - 3} + \dfrac{1}{N_2 - 3}}} = \frac{(.69) - (-.20)}{\sqrt{\dfrac{1}{12} + \dfrac{1}{97}}} = 2.91$$

as the Z of the difference between the two effect sizes. The p value associated with a Z of 2.91 is .002 one-tailed, or .004 two-tailed. We may conclude that these two effect sizes differ significantly.

Example 5. Studies A and B yield results in the same direction, with effect sizes of $r = .70$ (N = 20) and $r = .25$ (N = 95), respectively. The Fisher zs corresponding to these rs are .87 and .26, respectively. From equation 11, we obtain

$$\frac{z_1 - z_2}{\sqrt{\dfrac{1}{N_1 - 3} + \dfrac{1}{N_2 - 3}}} = \frac{(.87) - (.26)}{\sqrt{\dfrac{1}{17} + \dfrac{1}{92}}} = 2.31$$

as the Z of the difference. The p associated with that Z is .01 one-tailed, or .02 two-tailed. This example shows how two studies can agree that there is a significant positive relationship between variables X and Y but disagree statistically significantly in their estimates of the size of the relationship.

Example 6. Studies A and B yield effect-size estimates of $r = .00$ (N = 17) and $r = .30$ (N = 45), respectively. The Fisher zs corresponding to these rs are .00 and .31, respectively. From equation 11, we obtain

$$\frac{z_1 - z_2}{\sqrt{\dfrac{1}{N_1 - 3} + \dfrac{1}{N_2 - 3}}} = \frac{(.00) - (.31)}{\sqrt{\dfrac{1}{14} + \dfrac{1}{42}}} = -1.00$$

as the Z of the difference between our two effect size estimates. The p associated with that Z is .16 one-tailed, or .32 two-tailed. Here, we have an example of two effect sizes—one zero ($r = .00$), the other ($r = .30$) statistically significantly different from zero ($t(43) = 2.06$, $p < .025$ one-tailed) — that do not differ significantly. This well illustrates how careful we must be in concluding that results of two studies are heterogeneous when the effects of one are significant and the effects of the other are not or when one has a zero estimated effect size and the other does not.

Combining Studies

Significance Testing.
After we compare the results of any two independent studies, it is an easy matter also to combine the p levels of the two studies in order to get an overall estimate of the probability that the two p levels might have been obtained if the null hypothesis of no relationship between X and Y were true. Many methods for combining the results of two or more studies are available and have recently been summarized in detail (Rosenthal, 1978, 1980). Here, it is only necessary to describe the simplest and most versatile of the procedures, the method of adding Zs that Mosteller and Bush (1954) have called the *Stouffer method*. This method, like the method for comparing p values, asks us first to obtain accurate p levels for each of our two studies and then to find the Z that corresponds to each of these p levels. Both ps must be given in one-tailed form. The corresponding Zs will have the same sign if both studies show effects in the same direction, but they will have different signs if the results are in opposite directions. The sum of the two Zs, when divided by $\sqrt{2}$, yields a new Z that corresponds to the p value that the results of the two studies combined or that results even farther out in the same tail could have occurred if the null hypothesis of no relationship between X and Y were true. Recapping,

$$\frac{Z_1 + Z_2}{\sqrt{2}} \text{ is distributed as } Z. \tag{12}$$

Should we want to do so, we could weight each Z by its df (Rosenthal, 1978, 1980).

Example 7. Studies A and B yield results in opposite directions, and both are significant. One p is .05 one-tailed; the other p is .0000001, one-tailed but in the opposite direction. The Zs corresponding to these ps are found in a table of normal deviates to be -1.64 and 5.20, respectively. (Note that the opposite signs indicate results in opposite directions.) Then, from equation 12, we obtain

$$\frac{Z_1 + Z_2}{\sqrt{2}} = \frac{(-1.64) + (5.20)}{1.41} = 2.52$$

as the Z of the combined results of studies A and B. The p value associated with a Z of 2.52 is .006 one-tailed, or .012 two-tailed. Thus, the combined p supports the more significant of the two results. If these were actual results, we would want to be very cautious in interpreting our combined p, because the two ps that we combined were so very significantly different from each other. We would try to discover the differences between studies A and B that could have led to results that were so significantly different.

Example 8. Studies A and B yield results in the same direction, but neither is significant. One p is .11, the other is .09, and their associated Zs are 1.23 and 1.34, respectively, From equation 12, we obtain

$$\frac{Z_1 + Z_2}{\sqrt{2}} = \frac{(1.23) + (1.34)}{1.41} = 1.82$$

as the combined Z. The p associated with that Z is .034 one-tailed, or .068 two-tailed.

Effect-Size Estimation. When we want to combine the results of two studies, we are as interested in the combined estimate of the effect size as we are in the combined probability. As in the case when we compared two effect-size estimates, we shall consider r as our effect-size estimate in combining effect sizes, although we recognize that many other estimates are possible (for example, Cohen's d or differences between proportions).

For each of the two studies to be combined, we compute r and the associated Fisher z, and we have

$$\frac{z_1 + z_2}{2} = \bar{z} \tag{13}$$

as the Fisher z corresponding to our mean r. We use an r-to-z or z-to-r table to look up the r associated with our mean $\bar{z}$. Alternatively we could find r from z from the following: $r = (e^{2z} - 1)/(e^{2z} + 1)$. Tables are preferable. Should we want to do so, we could weight each z by its df (Snedecor and Cochran, 1967).

Example 9. Studies A and B yield results in opposite directions, one $r = .80$, the other $r = -.30$. The Fisher zs corresponding to these rs are 1.10 and -0.31, respectively. From equation 13, we obtain

$$\frac{z_1 + z_2}{2} = \frac{(1.10) + (-0.31)}{2} = .395$$

as the mean Fisher z. From a z-to-r table, we find that a z of .395 is associated with an r of .38.

Example 10. Studies A and B yield results in the same direction, one $r = .95$, the other $r = .25$. The Fisher zs corresponding to these rs are 1.83 and .26, respectively. From equation 13, we obtain

$$\frac{z_1 + z_2}{2} = \frac{1.83 + .26}{2} = 1.045$$

as the mean Fisher z. From a z-to-r table, we find a z of 1.045 to be associated with an r of .78. Note that if we had averaged the two rs without first transforming them to Fisher zs, we would have found the mean r to be $(.95 + .25)/2 = .60$ — substantially less than .78. This illustrates that the use of Fisher's z gives heavier weight to rs that are farther from zero in either direction.

Three or More Studies

Although the procedures presented thus far enable us to do quite a lot in the way of comparing and combining the results of sets of studies, it often happens that we want to compare or combine the results of three or more studies of the same relationship. The purpose of this section is to generalize procedures given in the last section so that we can compare and combine the results of any number of studies.

Comparing Studies

Significance Testing. When we want to compare three or more p levels, we first find the standard normal deviate, Z, that corresponds to each p level. All p levels must be one-tailed. The corresponding Zs will have the same sign if all studies show effects in the same direction and different signs if the effects are in different directions. The statistical significance of the heterogeneity of the Zs can be obtained from χ^2 that is computed as follows (Rosenthal and Rubin, 1979a):

$$\sum_{j=1}^{K} (Z_j - \overline{Z})^2 \text{ is distributed as } \chi^2 \text{ with } K - 1 \ df \tag{14}$$

In this equation, Z_j is the Z for any one study, and $\overline{Z}$ is the mean of all the $\overline{Z}$s obtained.

Example 11. Studies A, B, C, and D yield one-tailed p values of .15, .05, .01, and .001, respectively. The results of study C, however, are in an opposite direction. From a normal table, we find that the Zs corresponding to the four p levels are 1.04, 1.64, -2.33, and 3.09. (Note the negative sign for the Z associated with the result in the opposite direction.) Then, from equation 14, we obtain

$$\sum_{j=1}^{K} (Z_j - \overline{Z})^2 = [(1.04) - (0.86)]^2 + [(1.64 - (0.86)]^2 + [(-2.33) - (0.86)]^2 + [(3.09) - (0.86)]^2 = 15.79$$

as our χ^2 value, which for $K - 1 = 4 - 1 = 3$ df is significant at $p = .0013$. Thus, the four p values that we have compared are clearly significantly heterogeneous. Beyond the question of whether the p levels of a given set differ significantly among themselves, we sometimes want to test specific hypotheses about which studies will show the more significant p levels. This can be done by computing contrasts among the obtained p levels (Rosenthal and Rubin, 1979a).

Effect-Size Estimation. Here, we want to assess the statistical heterogeneity of three or more effect-size estimates. Again, we restrict our discussion to r as the effect-size estimator, although analogous procedures are available for comparing such other effect-size estimators as d or differences between proportions (Rosenthal and Rubin, in press a).

For each of the three or more studies to be compared, we compute the effect size r, its associated Fisher z, and $N - 3$, where N is the number of sampling units on which each r is based. Then, the statistical significance of the heterogeneity of the rs can be obtained from a χ^2 that is computed as follows (Snedecor and Cochran, 1967):

$$\sum_{j=1}^{K} (N_j - 3)(z_j - \bar{z})^2 \text{ is distributed as } \chi^2 \text{ with } K - 1 \ df \tag{15}$$

In this equation, z_j is the Fisher z that corresponds to any r, and $\bar{z}$ is the weighted mean z, that is,

$$\sum_{j=1}^{K} (N_j - 3) z_j / \sum_{j=1}^{K} (N_j - 3) \tag{16}$$

Example 12. Studies A, B, C, and D yield effect sizes of $r = .70$ ($N = 30$), $r = .45$ ($N = 45$), $r = .10$ ($N = 20$), and $r = -.15$ ($N = 25$), respectively. The Fisher zs corresponding to these rs are found from tables to be .87, .48, .10, and $-.15$, respectively. The weighted mean z is found from equation 16 to be $[27(.87) + 42(.48) + 17(.10) + 22(-.15)]/[27 + 42 + 17 + 22] = 42.05/108 = .39$.

Then, from equation 15, we obtain,

$$\sum_{j=1}^{K} (N_j - 3)(z_j - \bar{z})^2 = 27(.87 - .39)^2 + 42(.48 - .39)^2 + 17(.10 - .39)^2 + 22(-.15 - .39) = 14.41$$

as our χ^2 value, which for $K - 1 = 3$ df is significant at $p = .0024$. Thus, the four effect sizes that we have compared are clearly significantly heterogeneous. As in the case of the set of p values, procedures are also available for computing contrasts among the obtained effect-size estimates (Rosenthal and Rubin, in press a).

Combining Studies

Significance Testing. After we compare the results of any set of three or more studies, it is an easy matter also to combine the *p* levels of the set of studies to get an overall estimate of the probability that the set of *p* levels could have been obtained if the null hypothesis of no relationship between *X* and *Y* was true. Of the many methods that are available, we present here only the generalized version of the method presented earlier in the section on combining the results of two groups (Rosenthal, 1978, 1980).

This method requires only that we obtain *Z* for each of our *p* levels, all of which should be one-tailed. *Z*s disagreeing in direction from the majority of the findings are given negative signs. Then, the sum of the *Z*s, divided by the square root of the number (K) of studies, yields a new statistic distributed as *Z*. Symbolically,

$$\sum_{j=1}^{K} Z_j/\sqrt{K} \text{ is distributed as } Z \tag{17}$$

Should we want to do so, we could weight each of the *Z*s by its *df* (Rosenthal, 1978, 1980).

Example 13. Studies A, B, C, and D yield one-tailed *p* values of .15, .05, .01, and .001, respectively. The results of study C, however, are in an opposite direction. The four *Z*s associated with these four *p*s, then, are 1.04, 1.64, – 2.33, and 3.09. From equation 17, we obtain

$$\sum_{j=1}^{K} Z_j/\sqrt{K} = \frac{(1.04)+(1.64)+(-2.33)+(3.09)}{\sqrt{4}} = 1.72$$

as our new *Z* value, which has an associated *p* value of .043 one-tailed, or .086 two-tailed. This combined *p* supports the results of the majority of the individual studies. However, even if these two *p* values (.043 and .086) were more significant, we would want to be very cautious about drawing any simple overall conclusion, because of the very great heterogeneity of the four *p* values that we are combining. Example 11, which employed the same *p* values, showed that this heterogeneity was significant at *p* = .0013.

Effect-Size Estimation. When we combine the results of three or more studies, we are as interested in the combined estimate of the effect size as we are in the combined probability. We follow here our earlier procedure of considering *r* as our effect-size estimator while recognizing that many other estimates are possible. For each of the three or more studies to be combined, we compute *r* and the associated Fisher *z*, and we have

$$\sum_{j=1}^{K} z/K = \bar{z} \qquad (18)$$

as the Fisher $\bar{z}$ corresponding to our mean r. We use a table of Fisher z values to find the r associated with our mean $\bar{z}$. Should we want to do so, we could weight each z by its df (Snedecor and Cochran, 1967).

Example 14. Studies A, B, C, and D yield effect sizes of $r = .70, .45, .10,$ and $- .15$, respectively. The Fisher z values corresponding to these rs are $.87,$ $.48, .10,$ and $- .15$, respectively. Then, from equation 18, we obtain

$$\sum_{j=1}^{K} z/K = \frac{(.87) + (.48) + (.10) + (- .15)}{4} = .32$$

as our mean Fisher z. From a table of Fisher z values, we find that a z of .32 corresponds to an r of .31. As in example 13, however, we want to be very cautious in our interpretation of this combined effect size. If the rs that we have just averaged were based on substantial sample sizes, as they were in Example 12, they would be significantly heterogeneous, and averaging without special thought and comment would be inappropriate.

Practical Validity

So far, we have seen how we can better evaluate the results of a single study by always reporting an effect-size estimate as well as an accurate p value. We have also seen how we can compare and combine the p values and effect sizes of two or more studies in order to evaluate better what the accumulating evidence shows. In this section, we will discuss the interpretation of our effect-size estimators.

Despite a growing awareness of the importance of estimating effect sizes, there is a problem in evaluating various effect-size estimators from the point of view of practical usefulness. Rosenthal and Rubin (1979b, in press b) found that neither experienced behavioral researchers nor experienced statisticians had a good intuitive feel for the practical meaning of such common effect-size estimators as r^2, omega^2, epsilon^2, and similar estimates.

Accordingly, Rosenthal and Rubin introduced an intuitively appealing general-purpose effect-size display whose interpretation is perfectly transparent: the binomial effect-size display (BESD). While they do not claim to have resolved the differences and controversies surrounding the use of various effect-size estimators, they argue that their display is useful for three reasons: It is easily understood by researchers, students, and laypersons; it is applicable in a wide variety of contexts; and it is convenient to compute.

The question addressed by BESD is this: What is the effect on the success rate (for example, survival rate, cure rate, improvement rate, selection rate) of the institution of a new treatment procedure? Therefore, BESD displays the change in success rate (for example, survival rate, cure rate, improvement rate, selection rate) that can be attributed to the new treatment procedure. One example will show the appeal of the display.

In one of their meta-analyses of psychotherapy outcome studies, Smith and Glass (1977) summarized the results of some 400 studies. An eminent critic stated that the results of their analysis sounded the death knell for psychotherapy because of the modest size of the effect. This modest effect size was calculated to be equivalent to an r of .32, which accounted for only 10 percent of the variance.

Table 2 is the BESD corresponding to an r of 32 or an r^2 of .10. Table 2 shows clearly that it is absurd to label as "modest indeed" an effect size equivalent to increasing the success rate from 34 percent to 66 percent (for example, by reducing a death rate from 66 percent to 34 percent). Even so small an r as .20, which would account for only 4 percent of the variance, is associated with an increase in success rate from 40 percent to 60 percent — or with a decrease in death rate from 60 percent to 40 percent, which is hardly a trivial decrease.

One great convenience of the binomial effect-size display is the ease with which we can covert it to r (or r^2) and the ease with which we can go from r (or r^2) to the display.

Table 3 shows the systematic increase in success rates associated with various values of r^2 and r. For example, an r of .30, which accounts for only 9 percent of the variance, is associated with a reduction in death rate from 65 percent to 35 percent. The last column of Table 3 shows that the difference in success rates is identical to r. Consequently, the experimental group success rate in the BESD is computed as $.50 + r/2$, whereas the control group success rate is computed as $.50 - r/2$. Procedures for obtaining r from various tests of significance have been given in this chapter as equations 5, 6, and 7.

Rosenthal and Rubin (in press a) propose that use of the BESD can make the reporting of effect sizes both more intuitive and more informative. It is their belief that use of the BESD to display the increase in success rate due to

Table 2. The Binomial Effect-Size Display (BESD): An Example Accounting for Only 10 Percent of the Variance

| | Treatment Outcome | | |
	Benefited	Not Benefited	Σ
Treatment Condition	66	34	100
Control Condition	34	66	100
Σ	100	100	200

Table 3. Binomial Effect-Size Displays Corresponding to
Various Values of r^2 and r

r^2	r	Success Rate Increased From	To	Difference in Success Rates
.01	.10	.45	.55	.10
.04	.20	.40	.60	.20
.09	.30	.35	.65	.30
.16	.40	.30	.70	.40
.25	.50	.25	.75	.50
.36	.60	.20	.80	.60
.49	.70	.15	.85	.70
.64	.80	.10	.90	.80
.81	.90	.05	.95	.90
1.00	1.00	.00	1.00	1.00

treatment more clearly conveys the real-world importance of treatment effects than the more common descriptions of effect size as proportion of variance accounted for.

It could appear that the BESD can be employed only when the outcome variable is dichotomous, but that is not the case. It can be shown that, for many distributions, the agreement between the correlation p (the treatment variable correlated with the continuously distributed outcome variable) and the correlation ϕ (the treatment variable correlated with the dichotomized outcome variable) is quite good (Rosenthal and Rubin, in press b).

One potential effect of routine use of a display procedure like the BESD to index the practical validity of our research results is more useful and realistic assessments of how well we are doing in the behavioral and social sciences. Use of the BESD has, in fact, shown that we have been doing considerably better in the behavioral and social sciences than we thought.

References

Cohen, J. "The Statistical Power of Abnormal-Social Psychological Research: A Review." *Journal of Abnormal and Social Psychology*, 1962, *65*, 145–153.

Cohen, J. *Statistical Power Analysis for the Behavioral Sciences.* (Rev. ed.) New York: Academic Press, 1977.

Federighi, E. T. "Extended Tables of the Percentage Points of Students' *t*-Distribution." *Journal of the American Statistical Association*, 1959, *54*, 683–688.

Friedman, H. "Magnitude of Experimental Effect and a Table for Its Rapid Estimation." *Psychological Bulletin*, 1968, *70*, 245–251.

Glass, G. V. "Summarizing Effect Sizes." In R. Rosenthal (Ed.), *New Directions for Methodology of Social and Behavioral Science: Quantitative Assessment of Research Domains*, no. 5. San Francisco: Jossey-Bass, 1980.

Hall, J. A. "Gender Differences in Nonverbal Communication Skills." In R. Rosenthal (Ed.), *New Directions for Methodology of Social and Behavioral Science: Quantitative Assessment of Research Domains*, no. 5. San Francisco: Jossey-Bass, 1980.

Hsu, L. M. "Tests of Differences in p Levels as Tests of Differences in Effect Sizes." *Psychological Bulletin*, 1980, *88*, 705–708.

Mosteller, F. M., and Bush, R. R. "Selected Quantitative Techniques." In G. Lindzey (Ed.), *Handbook of Social Psychology*. Vol. 1: *Theory and Method*. Reading, Mass.: Addison-Wesley, 1954.

Pillemer, D. B., and Light, R. J. "Benefitting from Variation in Study Outcomes." In R. Rosenthal (Ed.), *New Directions for Methodology of Social and Behavioral Science: Quantitative Assessment of Research Domains*, no. 5. San Francisco: Jossey-Bass, 1980.

Rosenthal, R. "Combining Results of Independent Studies." *Psychological Bulletin*, 1978, *85*, 185–193.

Rosenthal, R. "Summarizing Significance Levels." In R. Rosenthal (Ed.), *New Directions for Methodology of Social and Behavioral Science: Quantitative Assessment of Research Domains*, no. 5. San Francisco: Jossey-Bass, 1980.

Rosenthal, R., and Gaito, J. "The Interpretation of Levels of Significance by Psychological Researchers." *Journal of Psychology*, 1963, *55*, 33–38.

Rosenthal, R., and Gaito, J. "Further Evidence for the Cliff Effect in the Interpretation of Levels of Significance." *Psychological Reports*, 1964, *15*, 570.

Rosenthal, R., and Rubin, D. B. "Interpersonal Expectancy Effects: The First 345 Studies." *The Behavioral and Brain Sciences*, 1978, *3*, 377–415.

Rosenthal, R., and Rubin, D. B. "Comparing Significance Levels of Independent Studies." *Psychological Bulletin*, 1979a, *86*, 1165–1168.

Rosenthal, R., and Rubin, D. B. "A Note on Percent Variance Explained as a Measure of the Importance of Effects." *Journal of Applied Social Psychology*, 1979b, *9*, 395–396.

Rosenthal, R., and Rubin, D. B. "Summarizing 345 Studies of Interpersonal Expectancy Effects." In R. Rosenthal (Ed.), *New Directions for Methodology of Social and Behavioral Science: Quantitative Assessment of Research Domains*, no. 5. San Francisco: Jossey-Bass, 1980.

Rosenthal, R., and Rubin, D. B. "Comparing Effect Sizes of Independent Studies." *Psychological Bulletin*, in press a.

Rosenthal, R., and Rubin, D. B. "A Simple, General-Purpose Display of Magnitude of Experimental Effect." *Journal of Educational Psychology*, in press b.

Smith, M. L. "Integrating Studies of Psychotherapy Outcomes." In R. Rosenthal (Ed.), *New Directions for Methodology of Social and Behavioral Science: Quantitative Assessment of Research Domains*, no. 5. San Francisco: Jossey-Bass, 1980.

Smith, M. L., and Glass, G. V. "Meta-Analysis of Psychotherapy Outcome Studies." *American Psychologist*, 1977, *32*, 752–760.

Snedecor, G. W., and Cochran, W. G. *Statistical Methods*. (6th ed.) Ames: Iowa State University Press, 1967.

Robert Rosenthal is professor of psychology in the Department of Psychology and Social Relations, Harvard University.

The rationale underlying convergent-discriminant validation is part of the basic logic of science.

Convergent-Discriminant Validation in Measurements and Research Strategies

Donald W. Fiske

The original exposition of convergent-discriminant validation (Campbell and Fiske, 1959) emphasized use of the multitrait-multimethod matrix as a procedure for examining the adequacy of tests and other methods for measuring traits. It paid less attention, however, to the set of concepts underlying the rationale for this procedure. This chapter will briefly consider how the procedure has fared in the last two decades and what the procedure has shown us about our methods and our constructs. Then, it will examine the concepts involved and discuss extensions of these concepts, their relationships to other validity constructs, and their fundamental role in the methodology of behavioral research. Reproducibility of measurements and findings is basic to science. The degree of reproducibility largely determines the degree of generalizability and our confidence in our generalizations. Given the prerequisite convergence among observations, we also need convergence between methods

The author is indebted to Donald T. Campbell, William D. Crano, Susan T. Fiske, William Wimsatt, and the editors for valuable comments on an earlier draft of this chapter.

D. Brinberg, L. Kidder (Eds.). *New Directions for Methodology of Social and Behavioral Science: Forms of Validity in Research*, no. 12. San Francisco: Jossey-Bass, June 1982.

and then convergence or generalizability over people, times, and other conditions. Such convergence, reproducibility, and generalizability are necessary to establish the discriminations and differences that enable us to make statements about relationships.

The Procedure for Evaluating a Trait-Method Unit

Social science badly needs to be able to evaluate both its methods and its constructs. Unlike the natural sciences, social science has many overlapping constructs — sets of two or more constructs with meanings that overlap to some extent, often to a very large extent. Although this condition is particularly evident in personality and related fields, it is also present elsewhere. Many of our constructs refer to fuzzy sets of dispositions or behaviors, where a few prototypical instances are surrounded by a multitude of elements that partake of the essence of each construct only to a degree (Fiske, 1978; for dominance as one example, see Buss and Craik, 1980). Unlike the constructs of mature natural sciences, the typical construct in social science is derived from lay thinking; it is a "natural" category (Rosch, 1978; Wiggins, in press).

Part of the problem stems from the inclusiveness of these constructs. Each has a range of diverse manifestations that cannot be fully encompassed by observations from a single perspective. Hence, no one method is sufficient to assess it. Moreover, as is well known, each method yields data infused with considerable variance specific to the particular instrument and to the general type of method. Most constructs used to make attributions to persons (for example, dominance, creativity, intelligence) are of this kind. The convergent-discriminant validation model is particularly well suited for assessing the adequacy both of such constructs and of the methods for measuring them as properties of persons. In contrast, constructs that refer to properties of brief, specific behavioral actions avoid this problem and can ordinarily be measured by a single method. Such concepts are at a much lower level of abstraction. Only an observer can identify a smile, a gesture, or a nod. There is no feasible alternative method. Such judgments require only convergence, that is, consensus among observers.

To appreciate the importance of this model, we have to examine a major gap in the methodology of social science. A science has to have norms for adequacy so that it can reach consensus in rejecting ideas, constructs, propositions, and methods. In matters of theory, Popper (1959) has emphasized that propositions must be testable and falsifiable. A statement that cannot be disproved in empirical work or even in principle has little value. Social science thinking is cluttered with questionable content — constructs and propositions — that endure because they cannot be rejected definitively. Given the imprecise nature of our constructs, it is very difficult or even impossible to devise a fully persuasive empirical test of a proposition that relates two constructs — a test that, if no relationship is observed in the data, compels most of us to conclude that the proposition is not correct. The multitrait-multimethod matrix can, however, provide grounds for rejecting a construct by demonstrating that the construct is not an entity that can be assessed in several ways or by showing that the construct cannot be discriminated from other constructs by any of the methods used.

We can reject a measuring instrument because we have pertinent criteria. That is, we can reject a measuring instrument when it does not have the dependability implied by the conceptualization of the property being measured. The method may show insufficient stability over time, inadequate internal consistency among items or other elements of the instrument, or excessive disagreement between independent observers who use the instrument. The multitrait-multimethod matrix provides an additional procedure for rejecting a measuring instrument, at least as a trait-method unit; that is, as a procedure for assessing a given trait. It can also be the basis for rejecting a method when the method yields data that do not converge with measurements from other methods or that do not discriminate among a set of constructs.

Using the Model. Although I have not systematically reviewed applications of the multitrait-multimethod model, I have the strong impression that almost all the published matrices resemble those of the 1959 paper (Campbell and Fiske, 1959). At best, they show modest convergence across methods and minimal discrimination among concepts. Rarely is no convergence found, but the absolute agreement between independent methods is almost always quite limited, and the very modest requirement of discrimination is almost never met for every trait-method unit involved. One excellent matrix (Jaccard, Weber, and Lundmark, 1975) owes its success to comparing fairly similar methods for assessing two quite distinct attitudes. Furthermore, we must realize that the published matrices are probably the best that have been developed. Unsatisfactory results are unlikely to be submitted, and even more unlikely to be accepted, for publication. Most such findings repose in file drawers (Rosenthal, 1979).

The published matrices show us that the method problem is still with us. It is particularly critical in the assessment of behavior where the products — the indices assigned to subjects — are themselves produced by the behavior of individual observers — either the subjects themselves or other persons. These products are generated by interpretations and inferences (Fiske, 1978), processes that lead to limited agreement among observers. Like other behavior, observational judgments can be affected by the general context (the meaning of the judgment situation to the observer), the particular instructions used, immediately preceding stimuli (questions or other items), and the specific content of the given stimulus, as well as by the postulated properties of the person being observed. Thus, the cognitive style and other aspects of the observer's personality can affect these judgments.

How should these matrices be analyzed? "We believe that a careful examination of a multitrait-multimethod matrix will indicate to the experimenter what his next steps should be: It will indicate which methods should be discarded or replaced, which concepts need sharper delineation, and which concepts are poorly measured because of excessive or confounding method variance" (Campbell and Fiske, 1959, p. 103). I continue to believe that direct inspection of each trait-method unit should be carried out in every instance. With a little thought and practice, the major interpretations of the matrix will become apparent to the investigator.

If the investigator wishes to go further, a number of analytic methods have been proposed. Several of these are reviewed by Ray and Heeler (1975), who show that these methods do not always converge on the same interpretations. Mellon and Crano (1977) review other methods and extend the approach to annual replications of a matrix. The analytic method that appears to be the most valuable was developed by Jöreskog (Jöreskog and Sörbom, 1979) as one form of his general model for the analysis of covariance structures. It yields answers to specific questions formulated by the investigator. It adds considerable objectivity and precision to the evaluation and interpretation of these matrices, especially by providing estimates of the trait, methods, and error variance in each measure. Lomax (1980) suggests that the Jöreskog method does not so much challenge the findings from careful inspection as it adds to them.

Once we have formed some judgment about the contributions of method variance to the scores from our several trait-method units, we are ready to make decisions about the next steps. Although we cannot eliminate the contributions of method variance, we can minimize them by selecting for future research the methods or trait-method units that have the smallest contributions. This tactic assumes that method contributions can be estimated dependably, that estimates for one set of data will predict well the values for other sets. This assumption seems questionable. For example, attempts to estimate the disposition to give socially desirable answers and to partial out the effects of this disposition on substantive scores have met with little success. Alternatively, we can form composite scores by combining the measurements obtained from methods that are as diverse and distinctive as possible. Our decision should be determined by the nature of the conceptual problem that is being attacked. This model serves us best when we use it not to evaluate the quality of data to be published but when we are tooling up at an early stage of research and making decisions about the methods and procedures to be employed in the study that we hope will be publishable.

The Underlying Rationale

Convergent-discriminant validation involves a rationale that adopts the correspondence meaning of validity, within the schema presented by Brinberg and McGrath in this volume. The basic terms are familiar: *constructs* (for attributes of persons) and *methods* (for observation of such properties). The rationale is simply that distinct methods for measuring a construct should show some degree of reproducibility and that these methods should discriminate appropriately between pairs of constructs.

How does this rationale relate to other validity concepts? Let us consider the aspect of construct validity that assesses the adequacy with which a construct has been operationalized. The first step in establishing such validity for a trait-method unit is demonstrating some convergence with other trait-method units in which the same trait is involved. (Since the original phrase, *trait-method unit*, may have inappropriately narrow connotations, other terms, such as *attribute-method unit*, will also be used in this chapter.) The investigator must determine that the unit does not yield measurements unique to that method. The definition of a construct should delineate the range of relevant methods. A general trait construct can be assessed from several perspectives, but a construct defined as a trait perceived by one category of observer can be assessed only from that perspective. Various procedures can be used to obtain the requisite perceptions. This consideration introduces the other side of construct validity, namely the validity or justification of the construct itself within its network of postulated relationships. Insofar as conceptualization of the construct states or implies that it is observable by different methods, such convergence must be shown empirically. Furthermore, insofar as the construct is taken as distinct from other, similar constructs, each construct-method unit should manifest appropriate discriminations separating it from others.

The other concepts applied to the validity of measuring instruments need no discussion here. Content validity is simply a matter of judging whether a given method for assessing a construct, and particularly the content used in that method, falls within the domain of that construct as implicitly conceived or explicitly specified. The two kinds of criterion-related validity, concurrent validity and predictive validity, involve the convergence between two trait-method units, the unit under examination and the unit that has already been accepted as adequate.

Internal and External Validity. What is the relationship between the rationale for convergent-discriminant validation and the concepts of internal and external validity? Since the last two terms were originally construed (Campbell, 1957), their meanings have evolved in the writings of Campbell (Campbell and Stanley, 1963; Cook and Campbell, 1979), and they have received other interpretations from other authors. What is important, however, is not the labels but the ideas. First, can the findings of an empirical investigation be given the interpretations made by the investigator?

For example, the investigator demonstrates that two arrays of measurements are correlated. Then, the investigator says that, since the numbers show that trait A, as measured by one trait-method unit, is related to trait B, as measured by the other trait-method unit, trait A is related to trait B. The acceptability of this interpretation must be determined in the light of a basic proposition underlying convergent-discriminant validation: Method variance is pervasive, ubiquitous. Almost invariably in social and behavioral science, each array of measurements from a construct-method unit contains variance associated with the method. Any obtained relationship between two such units can be due to method variance shared by both. To illustrate, the two methods may evoke the same response set, such as social desirability. More generally, however, two sets of measurements obtained from the same situation, such as the same testing session or the same laboratory experiment, share a common determinant that stems from the subjects' differential reactions to the same overall context. Confidence in an observed relationship is increased when the relationship is replicated by methods that are largely independent of each other.

In evaluating each concept-method unit used in an investigation, it must be recognized that the term *method* encompasses potential influences at several levels of abstraction. Taking a paper-and-pencil instrument as an example, these influences include the content of the items, the response format, the general instructions and other features of the test-task as a whole, the characteristics of the examiner, other features of the total setting, and the reason why the subject is taking the test. Two units that have any one of these elements in common can show convergence due to that source, so the relationship obtained between them cannot safely be interpreted as associated with the traits or constructs in those units. For any single investigation, the only certain protection against this threat to validity is units using completely independent methods. In principle, a major portion of social and behavioral research is subject to this potent threat.

That interpretation of independence between methods is operational. That is, two methods are independent when their applications involve no common element. Another kind of independence examines the rationale or theory underlying the measures. In principle, interest in a particular subject, such as art, can be assessed by a test of knowledge about art, but it can also be assessed by counting factual statements about art in a person's conversations or other free productions. These two methods are experimentally and operationally independent, but they share the same rationale: Knowledge about a topic indicates an interest in it. The same principle or assumption underlies both methods. In behavioral science, this matter seems best handled by establishing several subconcepts, such as interest in art as assessed by direct observation of behavior.

An underlying point in the preceding discussion deserves to be made explicit. Different methods for measuring any construct involve different psychological processes. The point is obvious when two methods use different types of observers, such as self-reports versus peer ratings. It is also obvious when a procedure asking for preferences and interests is contrasted with a procedure that asks for acquired information. A little thought shows that it also holds for procedures that differ in format, even when the difference is only in content, in the stimuli or items. Different items can elicit separate kinds of retrieving and cognizing processes. The corollary to this is that different psychological processes typically generate responses that, while possibly intercorrelated, are clearly not interchangeable.

Another criterion for the empirical study can be formulated as a question: Is the study reproducible? This question poses another: What does *reproducibility* mean? Reproducibility can refer to the representativeness of the sample of subjects used. That is, if the investigator composes another sample, will the findings be the same? Reproducibility can also refer to the experimental conditions or treatments. That is, does the report of the study give enough information that another investigator can replicate the conditions, and can another investigator duplicate the measuring operations? A third aspect of reproducibility deals with the observations or measurements: Can they be duplicated on the same subjects?

Reproducibility of measurements is especially important. Underlying convergent validation is the degree of agreement between measurements from two-trait method units. The literature clearly supports the proposition that the more distinct and independent the two methods, the lower the agreement between their scores. (In fact, a survey of seventy published matrices by Turner [1981] shows that both convergent validity and discriminant validity decrease with greater independence of method.) In general, the lower the correlation between the two units, the greater the likelihood that the relationships between each unit and other variables are not the same. Hence, in a study that uses two independent methods to assess a construct, it is very likely that the two sets of obtained relationships between that construct and other variables will not converge closely. This becomes even more probable when either or both units fail to discriminate the construct at issue from similar constructs (provided the units are not confounded with the same related constructs).

The preceding discussion has been concerned with the extent to which measurements and obtained relationships can be found or expected in investigations that are intended to reproduce the original investigation. Another important question involves the generalizability of relationships found between the variables that go beyond the specifications of the original study. Suppose that a study finds that trait-method unit a is related to unit b. The typical investigator will conclude that construct A and construct B, the traits or properties in units a and b, respectively, are related. The investigator must also decide the population of subjects for which that relation can be presumed to hold and the range of settings within which observations or measurements can be made. Any relationship in science holds only for a certain set of boundary conditions. All other aspects of generalizability depend upon the extent to which findings from the given methods for indexing constructs A and B can be generalized to other methods for assessing those constructs. Hence, the rationale for convergent-discriminant validation is involved in all matters of generalizability.

Extensions of the Basic Rationale

The original paper on convergent-discriminant validation (Campbell and Fiske, 1959) focused on individual differences with respect to traits. The term *trait* referred to such attributes of persons as abilities and personality characteristics. The term *method* was used in a fairly broad sense that included tests, types of observer, and measuring procedures in experiments. The basic rationale developed in that paper can be applied much more widely. The possibilities of the general convergent-discriminant approach have been developed by Paisley, Collins, and Paisley (1970). They identify a set of components or facets: concepts, measures, populations, times, and analysis models. They show that any two of these can be compared and contrasted in a convergent-discriminant matrix, the correlations being over instances of one of the remaining components. I will build on and modify their significant basic conceptualization without using their terms and definitions.

The general design involves identifying two facets of interest, such as traits and methods, and selecting several elements for each. Then, each element from one facet is combined with each element of the other facet, as in the concept-method unit. A measure of correlation or correspondence between each pair of units is calculated over some replication, such as persons. The replications are elements of some other facet.

One form of the general multi X-multi Y approach is multiperson-multioccasion, with correspondence over attributes being assessed. Presented as a matrix, the headings for the columns are:

	Subject X			*Subject Y*			*Subject Z*		
Occasions	1	2	3	1	2	3	1	2	3

and the rows have the same headings. In a study published in the same year as the paper by Campbell and Fiske (1959), Fiske and Van Buskirk (1959) compared Q-sort descriptions, based on sentence completion protocols, for several persons tested several times. The two facets were persons and trials, the correlation being over traits. For each judge separately, we found fair convergence among trials for the same person but poor discrimination between persons, the results holding both for a group of students and for a group of patients.

Another form is multiperson-multimethod, also with correspondence over attributes. Correspondence and discrimination for personality profiles from different sources (methods) have been examined by Harris (1980). For Bourne (1977), the elements of method were different observers:

	Observer X			Observer Y			Observer Z		
Targets	1	2	3	1	2	3	1	2	3

He had members of small groups describe other members, his facets being persons and observers, with correspondences assessed over descriptive items. He found that correspondence on the same person only slightly exceeded correspondence between different persons. That is, convergence on each person was not much better than lack of discrimination due to unwanted convergence between persons. The finding was repeated in each of three groups. This study illustrates that the general design need not be restricted to correlation coefficients as the indices of association or correspondence. The measurement scales can be nominal or categorical as well as ordinal, equal-interval, or ratio.

Note that the investigator's interest in the two facets being varied is not the same in each design. In the trait-method case, the investigator hopes to support the presumption that each trait is distinct and can be identified by more than one method and that each method serves its instrumental function without distorting the observed relationships. For the person-time case, the investigator is concerned with the persons and hopes that the effect of the particular time of measurement as it interacts with the person will be minimal.

Person-method and person-time are only two of the ten possible pairings of the five components identified by Paisley, Collins, and Paisley (1970). They present actual or hypothetical studies illustrating the other forms of the general approach, and their examples serve to remind the reader that the basic rationale extends far beyond the field of individual differences. For instance, the pairing of concepts and chronological dates can be found in survey panel studies, where the cross-lagged correlations between different variables at different times are of particular interest:

	Time X			Time Y			Time Z		
Variables	1	2	3	1	2	3	1	2	3

The variable-time pairing illustrates the fact that the basic design can be extended to investigations that focus not on the validity of an attribute-method unit but on the existence or form of a relationship. For instance, if one facet is method of analysis, the investigator could ask whether a relationship is stronger for rank correlation than for product-moment correlation or whether it is nonlinear rather than linear. Thus, as Paisley and her colleagues point out, the interest can lie more in discriminations than in convergences. In all these variations on the basic design, however, as in research designs generally, there is replication over one facet — typically over persons but in other instances over time or, as in profile correlations, over variables.

When the emphasis is on convergence, the study is usually methodological, and the investigator is checking the adequacy of methods or the stability over time. In methodological studies, however, there is also a concern for discrimination — between concepts, persons, or groups. When the emphasis is on discrimination, the study is likely to be substantive, and the investigator looks for differences — between cross-lagged correlations, for example. Any study, of course, can be both methodological and substantive. Thus, any substantive finding can be pertinent to the validity of a construct. There seems to be little point in making a sharp categorical distinction between the two kinds of research. Certainly, the question of generalizability of findings does not fall exclusively into one or the other of these categories. Consider, for instance, a study of the generalizability (convergence) of findings across to distinct populations.

The Generalization of Convergence and Discrimination

Although discriminant validation applies to a broad domain, that domain is circumscribed by two pervasive features of social and behavioral measurement: the use of observers and the breadth of the concepts studied. There is no difficulty in discriminating between concepts when they refer to actions conceptualized at low levels of abstraction, such as "presses bar," "drinks," or "nods, gesticulates." The problem of discrimination enters with concepts like assertion, aggression, extraversion, and self-confidence. Where concepts are global and there is potential overlap and where concepts must be judged by observers who make inferences from manifested behaviors, the investigator must be concerned with discriminant validation (Fiske, 1978). Problems raised by Shweder and D'Andrade (1980) are pertinent here, too.

A given pair of personality variables can be seen as overlapping, as covarying, or both. How does one distinguish overlap from covariation? Do nurturance and affiliation overlap in their definitions, or do they covary in their judged strengths? Whatever the interpretation, researchers have expended much effort in assessing the relationships between such variables. Although the usual question is simply whether the variables are related, researchers often want to decide whether two variables have a strong or a weak relationship. Such determination cannot be made with confidence from a study that uses a single method. For the same group of subjects or for different groups of subjects, two methods can yield quite different levels of relationship, although the methods are fairly similar (Fiske, 1973). Thus, the determination of a construct's pattern of relationships (positive, negative, or absent) that is required for judging construct validity is threatened if not prevented by method variance.

Multiple Operations and Triangulation. Campbell (1969) has argued that we cannot avoid the confounding effects of method on our measurements; that is, method variance is ubiquitous. Given fallible measurements, our recourse must be to multiple operations. That is, we must measure a given property by a set of methods as different and independent as possible, and the methods must be selected so that they have as little in common as possible. By this triangulation, Campbell says, we get at the construct of interest in the best way we can. Variance associated with the construct is maximized, while the unwanted contributions from methods tend to counteract one another. This strategy has the same general form as the rationale for classical test theory, in which the observed scores for items are postulated as containing true variance plus error. The summing of such scores yields a reliable total score, because the true variance accumulates, while the error variances of the individual items tend to cancel one another out, since, in principle, they are uncorrelated. (The concept of triangulation and its ramifications are examined by Crano, 1981, who presents guidelines for applying it.)

The strategy of using multiple operations seems like an attractive solution to the problem of method variance. However, we lack a definitive set of tactics for carrying it out. In most instances, an investigator can identify two or more methods for measuring each construct of interest, but what is to be done next? If the scores obtained by these methods are to be combined, should they have equal weight, or should they be weighted by the investigator's judgment of their relative value as indicants of the construct? Again, how many methods are needed to assess the construct adequately? Should we be satisfied with two or three distinct methods, or should we make an effort to use so many methods that every aspect, every manifestation of the construct is covered by one or more methods?

To be realistic, no one is going to attempt a complete assessment of any single construct by using all possible methods and including all pertinent manifestations of the construct. Probably no construct used in social science has been completely described, so there is not a complete listing that specifies every kind of behavior that partakes of the construct to any degree. Perhaps the most extensive descriptions of constructs are those developed by Murray (1938), yet these do not state the methods by which the manifestations are to be observed. In other words, no one will ever actualize a complete universe score of the kind defined by Cronbach and others (1972) as the mean of all acceptable observations under all allowable conditions of measurement.

Accepting the limitations imposed by the fuzzy constructs in social science, the typical investigator is realistic and selects two or three fairly distinct methods that seem adequate psychometrically. The investigator's way of combining scores from these methods, such as adding the standard scores, will ordinarily be chosen on a priori, intuitive grounds. In response to skeptics, the investigator is apt to reply that this procedure will do and that it is at least as good as standard practice in the professional community.

Convergent-discriminant validation was developed in the context of work on individual differences. Hence, it is of particular concern for the correlational discipline of scientific psychology (Cronbach, 1957). Procedures based on that rationale are usually not needed in experimental psychology, and they may not even be applicable there. In particular, the problem of attribute-method confounding is less critical in experimental psychology. The experimentalist is less ambitious than the correlationalist and does not seek to assign attributes to persons as entities but rather pursues the more limited objective of observing properties of behaviors. Yet, experimental work does have to deal with method specificity and method variance. How does one measure memory, learning, or reading comprehension? Furthermore, the independent variable and the dependent variable should not share variance from common features of the methods used to measure them. In a study of children in free play, the same observer should not be used to judge the aggressiveness of one child's acts and to code the subsequent responses of other children.

Convergence is of concern with respect to the dependent variable. Frequently, a single method for measuring it is not sufficient, and the experimenter must devise additional independent methods. For example, Rosch (1978) reports the use of four converging operational definitions in work on level of abstraction in categorization. Also, questions are frequently raised about the experimental manipulation. Does it adequately capture the underlying construct of interest? Experimenters often demonstrate the dependability of their effect by showing that it is found with alternative manipulations. This tactic also guards against the possibility that the effect is associated with some unrecognized aspect of the procedure used to produce varying levels of the independent variable.

Convergent Operations and Convergent Determinations. The ideal programmatic strategy in science seems to be use of convergent operations (Garner, 1974; Garner, Hake, and Eriksen, 1956). In the most general form, this means that a given problem or phenomenon is investigated by a diverse set of research programs that have few or no procedures in common. The various programs can approach the target from diverse perspectives. When the findings obtained from these independent attacks converge, the investigator can draw conclusions with a high degree of confidence. Although it is well to keep this ideal in mind, the typical behavioral scientist today cannot pursue it. This strategy is really available only when a field has advanced to a point where phenomena can be well delineated or problems can be formulated fairly precisely. Much social and behavioral science is still seeking to identify its phenomena objectively. In addition, the field lacks the body of established constructs that seem necessary for clear specification of the problems to be investigated.

The use of convergent operations applies the convergent-discriminant strategy on a large scale. Yet, an investigator who is fortunate enough to have the resources to utilize that grand strategy must still be cautious in drawing general conclusions. Suppose that two separate programs find that two constructs are related. It is quite possible that the finding of each program comes from method variance. Although the confounding method variance in the two studies is different, the biasing effects can be in the same direction. Of course, it is less likely that this coincidence will occur than it is that there will be bias in each study, but it is at least possible, and it can be appreciable. (For an analysis of problems posed by shared biases and assumptions in work on biological selection, see Wimsatt, 1980).

The pervasiveness of convergence has been brought out by Wimsatt (1981) in his work on robustness. He demonstrates the fundamental role of robustness in both the conceptual and the operational philosophy of science. We get at the real by its robustness over ways of knowing. We seek convergences among measuring operations. We derive the same result or theorem by different models or sets of assumptions. Thus, robustness is invariance over multiple means of determination.

We see, then, that convergent-discriminant validation by the multitrait-multimethod matrix is only one instance of a class of multi X-multi Y matrices or designs. Such matrices bring out the fundamental roles of the concepts of convergence and discrimination. Science seeks discriminations or differences. "Knowledge is knowledge of differences" (Runkel and McGrath, 1972, p. 37). Science also seeks relationships, but relationships can be construed as corresponding differences: A difference in one variable is associated with a difference in another variable. Hence, as noted earlier, the substantive side of science is concerned with discriminations. The methodological side of science, however, insists on replication and dependability. These properties can be studied in matrix form or by other analytical procedures. Within any one method of data collection, there must be congruence among observations of the given property in the objects or persons being studied, as in the classical forms of reliability. Next, there must be convergence toward agreement between methods, as in multimethod matrices. After the adequacy of methods has been established, it is necessary to demonstrate empirically, not just to argue a priori, that the findings of a study hold within some domain; that is, within a designated set of boundaries that identify explicit objects (persons), properties, and contexts (states of other variables). This last, crucial, stage which is often identified as external validity, involves both convergence or regularity within the domain of relevant phenomena and discrimination of that domain from all other domains.

It is important to recognize that many levels of correspondence have been considered in this chapter. For the multitrait-multimethod matrix, the first criterion stated was simply some convergence — correlations above zero. Similarly, modest agreement between the findings of different studies may be acceptable at the present stage of development of behavioral science. In contrast, observations of the same phenomenon should correspond so highly that they are essentially congruent. In thinking about correspondence, we must consider whether the degree is appropriate for the methodological question being asked.

Conclusion

The rationale underlying convergent-discriminant validation is part of the basic logic of science. The particular applications presented in the original paper (Campbell and Fiske, 1959) and published in many subsequent reports demonstrate the need for the explicit formulation and empirical examination of our substantive constructs. The nature of the phenomena studied in social science and the ways in which these phenomena have been construed made the analysis and study of convergence and discrimination inevitable and even necessary. The concept of construct validity has a similar history. As Cronbach and Meehl (1955) point out, the ideas that underlie it have always been part of scientific method. Yet, the concept had to be made explicit to help social and behavioral scientists deal with the kind of broad construct that is so prevalent in their field.

The original model of convergent-discriminant validation is weak. Its very modest criteria are appropriate for the current state of much social science, since they provide challenges that are often not met by current methods and constructs. Even if the day comes when these requirements are so routinely satisfied that an investigator no longer needs to publish matrices demonstrating the adequacy of the methods used, most social science will still have a long way to go. The first goals must be to obtain very high degrees of convergence among observations, among methods, and among findings and marked correspondence among interpretations of results. A mature science requires very close replicability as a foundation for its agreed-upon core of findings and laws. The ultimate goal must be convergence not only across diverse methods of measurement but also across separate research strategies. The objective should be the formulation of laws that are not restricted by the investigator's particular approach.

References

Bourne, E. "Can We Describe an Individual's Personality? Agreement on Stereotype Versus Individual Attributes." *Journal of Personality and Social Psychology,* 1977, *5,* 863-872.

Buss, D. M., and Craik, K. H. "The Frequency Concept of Disposition: Dominance and Prototypically Dominant Acts." *Journal of Personality,* 1980, *48,* 379-392.

Campbell, D. T. "Factors Relevant to the Validity of Experiments in Social Settings." *Psychological Bulletin,* 1957, *54,* 297-312.

Campbell, D. T. "Definitional Versus Multiple Operationalism." *et. al.,* 1969, *2,* 14-17.

Campbell, D. T., and Fiske, D. W. "Convergent and Discriminant Validation by the Multitrait-Multimethod Matrix." *Psychological Bulletin,* 1959, *56,* 81-105.

Campbell, D. T., and Stanley, J. C. "Experimental and Quasi-Experimental Designs for Research on Teaching." In N. L. Gage (Ed.), *Handbook of Research on Teaching.* Chicago: Rand McNally, 1963. Reprinted separately as *Experimental and Quasi-Experimental Designs for Research.* Chicago: Rand McNally, 1966.

Cook, T. D., and Campbell, D. T. *Quasi Experimentation: Design and Analysis Issues for Field Settings.* Chicago: Rand McNally, 1979.

Crano, W. D. "Triangulation and Cross-Cultural Research." In M. B. Brewer and B. E. Collins (Eds.), *Scientific Inquiry and the Social Sciences: A Volume in Honor of Donald T. Campbell.* San Francisco: Jossey-Bass, 1981.

Cronbach, L. J. "The Two Disciplines of Scientific Psychology." *American Psychologist,* 1957, *12,* 671-684.

Cronbach, L. J., Gleser, G. C., Nanda, H., and Rajaratnam, N. *The Dependability of Behavioral Measurements: Theory of Generalizability for Scores and Profiles.* New York: Wiley, 1972.

Cronbach, L. J., and Meehl, P. E. "Construct Validity in Psychological Tests." *Psychological Bulletin,* 1955, *52,* 281-302.

Fiske, D. W. "Can a Personality Construct Be Validated Empirically?" *Psychological Bulletin,* 1973, *80,* 89-92.

Fiske, D. W. *Strategies for Personality Research: The Observation Versus Interpretation of Behavior.* San Francisco: Jossey-Bass, 1978.

Fiske, D. W., and Van Buskirk, C. "The Stability of Interpretations of Sentence Completion Protocols." *Journal of Consulting Psychology,* 1959, *23,* 177-180.

Garner, W. R. *The Processing of Information and Structure.* Hillsdale, N.J.: Erlbaum, 1974.

Garner, W. R., Hake, H. W., and Eriksen, C. W. "Operationism and the Concept of Perception." *Psychological Review,* 1956, *63,* 149-159.

Harris, J. G., Jr. "Nomovalidation and Idiovalidation: A Quest for the True Personality Profile." *American Psychologist,* 1980, *35,* 729-744.

Jaccard, J. J., Weber, J., and Lundmark, J. "A Multitrait-Multimethod Analysis of Four Attitude Assessment Procedures." *Journal of Experimental Social Psychology,* 1975, *11,* 149-154.

Jöreskog, K. G., and Sörbom, D. *Advances in Factor Analysis and Structural Equation Models.* Cambridge, Mass.: Abt, 1979.

Lomax, R. G. "Covariance Structure Analysis of Multitrait-Multimethod Matrices." Unpublished manuscript, University of Pittsburgh, 1980.

Mellon, P. M., and Crano, W. D. "An Extension and Application of the Multitrait-Multimethod Matrix Technique." *Journal of Educational Psychology,* 1977, *69,* 716-723.

Murray, H. A., and others. *Explorations in Personality.* New York: Oxford, 1938.

Paisley, M. B., Collins, W. A., and Paisley, W. J. "The Convergent-Discriminant Matrix: Multitrait-Multimethod Logic Extended to Other Social Research Decisions." Unpublished manuscript, Stanford University, 1970.

Popper, K. R. *The Logic of Scientific Discovery.* New York: Basic Books, 1959.

Ray, M. L., and Heeler, R. M. "Analysis Techniques for Exploratory Use of the Multrait-Multimethod Matrix." *Educational and Psychological Measurement,* 1975, *35,* 255–265.

Rosch, E. "Principles of Categorization." In E. Rosch and D. B. Lloyd (Eds.), *Cognition and Categorization.* Hillsdale, N.J.: Erlbaum, 1978.

Rosenthal, R. "The File Drawer Problem and Tolerance for Null Results." *Psychological Bulletin,* 1979, *86,* 638–641.

Runkel, P. J., and McGrath, J. E. *Research on Human Behavior: A Systematic Guide to Method.* New York: Holt, Rinehart and Winston, 1972.

Shweder, R. A., and D'Andrade, R. G. "The Systematic Distortion Hypothesis." In R. A. Shweder (Ed.), *New Directions for Methodology of Social and Behavioral Science: Fallible Judgment in Behavioral Research,* no. 4. San Francisco: Jossey-Bass, 1980.

Turner, C. J. "The Multitrait-Multimethod Matrix: 1967–1980." *JSAS Catalog of Selected Documents in Psychology,* 1981, *11,* 46 (Ms. #2280).

Wiggins, J. S. "Circumplex Models of Interpersonal Behavior in Clinical Psychology." In P. C. Kendall and J. N. Butcher (Eds.), *Handbook of Research Methods in Clinical Psychology.* New York: Wiley-Interscience, in press.

Wimsatt, W. C. "Reductionist Research Strategies and Their Biases in the Units of Selection Controversy." In T. Nickles (Ed.), *Scientific Discoveries: Case Studies.* Dordrecht, Holland: Reidel, 1980.

Wimsatt, W. "Robustness, Reliability, and Multiple Determination in Science." In M. B. Brewer and B. E. Collins (Eds.), *Scientific Inquiry and the Social Sciences: A Volume in Honor of Donald T. Campbell.* San Francisco: Jossey-Bass, 1981.

Donald W. Fiske is professor of psychology and chair of the Committee on Methodology of Behavioral Research, Department of Behavioral Sciences, University of Chicago.

A reexamination of some assumptions underlying the multitrait-multimethod strategy calls for radical gestalt shifts in our conceptualizations.

Methods as Diluting Trait Relationships Rather Than Adding Irrelevant Systematic Variance

Donald T. Campbell
Edward J. O'Connell

Fiske's review in this volume of the validity of personality measurement as seen through the multitrait-multimethod matrix correctly presents a very disappointing picture. We measure stable aspects of personality very poorly—if indeed there are any—but we do not recognize how poorly we measure them unless we compare different methods. Even when we find some evidence of both convergent and discriminant validity, the validity correlations are low and only slightly higher than the heterotrait-heteromethod values. Even when we have good evidence of both convergent and discriminant validity, we do not know how to combine these multiple images into a single personality description, either for a single person or as a portrait of the true trait relationships for the conceptual domain.

This chapter was supported in part by National Science Foundation Grant BNS 7925577. The authors have profited from suggestions made by David A. Kenny, Charles S. Reichardt, and Robert L. Linn.

D. Brinberg, L. Kidder (Eds.). *New Directions for Methodology of Social and Behavioral Science: Forms of Validity in Research*, no. 12. San Francisco: Jossey-Bass, June 1982.

Triangulation and binocular convergence were initially encouraging metaphors (Campbell, 1959, 1961, 1966; Campbell and Fiske, 1959), but in the personality domain we have not received the benefits that triangulation provides in binocular vision or in land surveys. For both, which, of course, are prime sources of the metaphor, triangulation results in both increased clarity and additional information about the depth dimension. The clarity provided is of two types, objectively valid clarification and subjective or perceived clarity. Visual triangulations usually provide both, except in extremely atypical situations, such as the stereoscope, in which perceived clarity is not always accompanied by objective clarification. Illusions of the latter sort, however, have to be contrived by a psychologist who knows the laws of vision. Haphazard degrading of visual information does not produce them. The rare occurrence in visual space perception of illusory clarity and illusory depth is not relevant to the disappointing results of triangulation in the study of personality. Methodological triangulation in the personality domain — using multiple methods with multiple traits — has greatly reduced subjectively perceived clarity. Moreover, even when the resulting matrix gives hints of triangulation on an objective reality, it does not pare away the irrelevant components and present us with an improved net picture.

One answer is, of course, that perhaps there are no such objects to be perceived — that no matter what ideal method we might use, no clarifying triangulation could result. The disappointment may be valid. Individuals can differ reliably in very specific settings, but the setting-person interactions are so strong that no trans-setting personality traits exist. (This was Robert Tryon's view after much work on individual differences in rats and humans. In his teaching Campbell about apparatus factors in rat research, Tryon is the grandfather of the multitrait-multimethod matrix.) Such a finding would correspond to the sociologist's dogma that behavior is to be predicted from social role and social setting, not from permanent traits that individual persons impose on all situations. Learning theory can lead to similar conclusions. If, for example, we were to have five rats concurrently learn five discriminable mazes to asymptotic accuracy, we would certainly be better able to predict the right-or-left turn at a given instant by knowing not which rat it is but which unit in which maze, if we cannot know both. Even if we were dealing with rats that have only half-learned the maze and that confuse it with another or if we are dealing with humans whose mazes, roles, and settings we only partially know, perhaps nothing like personality traits would emerge. These may be the correct conclusions from the experience that Fiske reviews. However, the degree to which we sometimes discover convergent and discriminant validity for generalized personality traits — even if the validity coefficients are only between .30 and .50 — leads us to suggest that this negative discovery may not be the whole story and that we should also consider putting the methodology on trial.

In this spirit, this chapter is intended to encourage a new generation of methodologists, perhaps with new techniques of spectral analysis borrowed from radio and space flight astronomy, to re-examine our problem of obtaining clearer images from noisy, static-ridden, and biased channels and to look for other means by which triangulation in the personality measurement domain can lead to greater clarity

This chapter proposes no definitive new answers, only some tentative suggestions aimed at provoking readers to re-examination of basic methodological assumptions.

The Empirical Puzzle

In an obscurely published and never cited (viz: Social Science Citation Index) paper, Campbell and O'Connell (1967) presented evidence of several kinds showing that methods factors interact in a specific multiplicative way with trait factors: The higher the basic relationship between two traits, the more that relationship is increased when the same method is shared. In contrast, if two traits are basically independent, their correlation is still essentially zero even when they are measured by the same method. We regarded this discovery as incompatible with the original conceptual bases of methods factors and factor analysis. We called upon the psychometric tradition to meet this challenge. We spent several frustrating years on computer simulations of the problem, but we published nothing more and have indeed even repressed and mislaid the details of the analyses that we did. While our paper has met with no published response, Allen Yates (1980) has addressed the issue by revising the conceptualization of simple structure in factor analysis. Yates' approach more closely resembles the kind of possible solution that we had in mind then than it does what we propose here, for it retains the notion that sharing the same method increases the correlations between two measures above the true relationship. The conceptual reversal that we will argue here is that not sharing the same method dilutes or attenuates the true relationship, so that it appears to be less than it should be. Fiske alludes to that possibility elsewhere in this volume (p. 83). We have come to this insight by another route. To present it, we need to backtrack. In Table 1, we present an example of the traditional factor analytic model that underlies both the original multitrait-multimethod matrix (Campbell and Fiske, 1959) and our 1967 paper (Campbell and O'Connell, 1967). The trait factors t, u, v, w, x, and so on are presumed to explain the nonindependence of the traits when method is not involved, that is, when correlations share no method, as in the heterotrait-heteromethod triangles. There are several method factors — m, n, o, p, q, and so forth. For now, and for most of our earlier imagery, each single method, M_1, M_2, . . . involves only a single methods factor; thus, methods are totally independent. (In Table 1A, zero loadings are left blank.)

Table 1. A Traditional Model Multitrait-Multimethod Matrix

1A — Factor Loadings

Measures		Trait Factors			Method Factors	
		t	u	v	m	n
Method 1	A_1	.50	.41	.31	.50	
	B_1		.70		.51	
	C_1			.80	.52	
Method 2	A_2	.51	.40	.30		.42
	B_2		.71			.41
	C_2			.81		.40

1B — Correlation Matrix

	A_1	B_1	C_1	A_2	B_2	C_2
A_1	(.76)					
B_1	.54	(.75)				
C_1	.51	.27	(.91)			
A_2	*.51*	.28	.24	(.69)		
B_2	.29	*.50*	.00	.46	(.67)	
C_2	.25	.00	*.65*	.41	.16	(.82)

In the multitrait-multimethod matrix illustrated in Table 1B, the reliability coefficients are placed in parentheses. These are the sum of the squares of the factor loadings for each measure, including, of course, the method factors. The other values are correlation coefficients between two separate measures; they are derived from the factor loadings as the sum of products of the loadings of the two variables on each factor. The validity values are italicized. The pattern of intertrait relationships is displayed in four triads of correlations, one within each method, and two that are independent of shared methods. In the jargon of Campbell and Fiske (1959), these four intertrait patterns are the two heterotrait-monomethod triangles and the two heterotrait-heteromethod triangles lying above and below the validity diagonal. Note that the two heterotrait-heteromethod triangles are not identical. The two correlations of A with B (A_1B_2 = .29 and A_2B_1 = .28) share no array of scores in common. The parallel values in Table 1A have been made trivially different so as to highlight this point.

While the matrix of Table 1B is not too different from the best examples of Campbell and Fiske (1959) and of the subsequent literature, the reader may well be appalled at the simplification laid bare by the chosen factor loadings. The trait factors are set almost identical for each method, and the methods loadings are set almost identical for the different traits. The manifest methods share no underlying method factors. Methods and traits are conceptualized as belonging to entirely separate and independent realms.

This conceptualization leads to the empirical puzzle examined in this chapter. At the risk of confusion, however, some parenthetical comments are in order. Campbell and Fiske (1959) regarded a matrix as not completely interpretable or decomposable if the lowest heterotrait-heteromethod correlations did not reach zero. This required both that one method was completely independent of a second method and that one trait was completely independent of a second trait. While they used mainly this very simple conceptualization, they also considered more complex possibilities. For example, they illustrated that traits and methods could reverse roles, turning a multitrait-multimethod matrix inside out. Degrees of similarity among methods (shared methods factors) were recognized and discussed, as in the gradations between ideal extremes of pure reliability, where both methods and traits were completely shared, and validity, where methods were entirely independent, and only traits were shared. However, the likelihood of a method that mixed both trait and method factors was not considered. There are the beginnings of such discussion in the context of response sets and the F scale of authoritarian personality (Campbell, Siegman, and Rees, 1967; Chapman and Campbell, 1957), and such complexity may seem needed where the two heterotrait-heteromethod triangles show asymmetry. However, many other possible and likely complexities remain totally unexplored, and they are worth considering before the radical solution offered here is accepted.

A Priori Expectations

Look at two parallel heterotrait triangles in Table1B: the monomethod triangle for Method 1 (with values of .54, .51, and .27) and the heteromethod triangle below the validity diagonal (with values of .29, .25, and .00). Both triangles show a very similar pattern of intertrait relationships. Traits A and B are the most closely related, and B and C, the least. The monomethod values are all higher, about .26 correlation points higher — the additive contribution in the monomethod values of their shared method factor. Figure 1A crudely plots this relationship for the three paired values. The three dots represent BC (.00 and .27), AC (.25 and .51), and AB (.29 and .54). Four such plots can be derived from each multitrait-multimethod matrix by pairing values from each of the heteromethod triangles with parallel values from each of the monomethod triangles.

It is apparent from Table 1A that, if we expanded this model to include more traits and thus many more heterotrait values, the scatter of points would lie parallel to the 45 degree line, which represents identical values and zero method-factor contribution. It is our anticipation that, were methods factors and trait factors randomly varied to a larger degree than in the overly idealized Table 1, this parallelism would continue, but with a larger scatter. This assumption needs more exploration, but it seems implicit in the combination of the additive model shared by all factor-analytic methods with the assumption that the method loading is independent of the trait loading. We employed, then as now, visually judged scatter plots in our argument, and we computed a net slope rather than the regression line of monomethod values on heteromethod values, since we wanted an index of slope that was independent of degree of scatter. If the regression were used, greater variability of trait loadings and method loadings across measures would increase the scatter and produce a flatter regression line, less than 45 degrees, less than a slope of 1.00.

In constructing a hypothetical example like Table 1 that starts from arbitrarily selected factor loadings, one is apt to be embarrassed by generating correlation coefficients larger than 1.00. This points to a major implausibility of the model. It would be much more realistic to start with a table of unstandardized components of variance and then to introduce a standardizing process. The overall result would cause those variables with the larger trait variance to have smaller method-factor loadings, since the contribution of methods to the total variance would be decreased. In general (although not in our arbitrary example of Table 1), variables with higher trait loadings produce higher intertrait correlations, and as a result their correlations are less enhanced when their measures share the same method. In general, intertrait correlations that were truly zero in the heteromethod triangle would increase more if method were shared than basically high intertrait relations would. If one were to consider a net slope measure that was independent of scatter, the expected slope on this basis would also be less than 45 degrees, less than 1.00.

Outcomes

The expectations raised by these a priori considerations (the first for slopes of 1.00 paralleling the identity diagonal, the second for slopes less than 1.00) are refuted by what we found. Slopes larger than 1.00 were the rule. Figure 1B shows data on staff and teammate ratings from the study by Kelly and Fiske (1951) as reanalyzed by Campbell and Fiske (1959). Figure 1B, like Figure 1A, is a scatter plot of intertrait correlation coefficients, expanded from three traits and three intertrait coefficients to include the 231 intertrait correlations among the twenty-two traits used in the study. Note, first, that the pattern of intertrait correlations is quite similar in the heteromethod triangle, where no shared method is involved, and in the monomethod triangle, where all traits are measured by the same raters. In fact, the correla-

Figure 1. Scatter Plots for Similarity of Monomethod and
Heteromethod Estimates of Intertrait Correlations

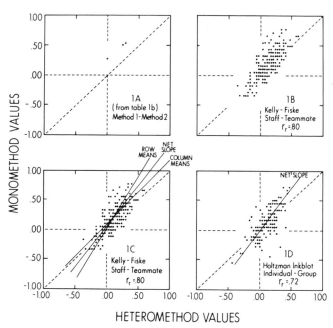

HETEROMETHOD VALUES

Note: In each case, the monomethod values are for the first method listed. (See text for explanation.)

tion r_r is .80. Note, too, that there is evidence of a method factor, in that the monomethod values average higher than the heteromethod values. Note the visual impression of slope: The intertrait correlations that are most augmented by being measured by the same raters are the larger ones. A basically zero intertrait relationship is zero, whether it is measured by the same rater or by different raters.

Figure 1C repeats the scatter plot of Figure 1B, but with the two standard regression lines and a net slope superimposed in order to introduce the scatterfree or net slope index that we will be using subsequently. Note, in judging the fit between the scatter points and the fitted lines, that the scatter plot program could put only one point in a cell, no matter how many cases fell there. The visual impression that results is sometimes misleading. In preparing the scatter plots, some variables were reflected, that is, they were reversed in sign to maximize the number of positive correlations. Where there were three methods, this was done separately for each pair. Only the two sets of monomethod values were used in making decisions on reflection. In Figure 1C, the line labeled *Column Means* is one of the two ordinary regression lines, to wit the best-fitting line predicting monomethod values from heteromethod values. For an eyeball fitting of such a line, imagine a best-fitting line that goes through the mean values for each column and gives heavier weight to the columns with more cases. The line labeled *Row Means* is the other standard regression line. The net slope is an intermediate slope, the line on which the two ordinary regression lines would converge if there were no scatter, that is, if the r_r were + 1.00. (This turns out to be the ratio of the two standard deviations plotted through the two means.) It is this net slope line that we will be using in what follows. Note that, in this case, the net slope passes close to the zero-zero axis.

Other Data. Figure 1D is included as the only case from our earlier paper (Campbell and O'Connell, 1967) that did not involve ratings. The data come from the experiment by Holtzman and others (1963), where 100 persons took the Holtzman Inkblot Test in both individual and group form. The responses were scored on eighteen variables. We find the same pattern again; in this case, the net slope intersects the zero-zero origin almost exactly. In our paper of 1967, there were seventeen matrices from eight separate studies, and four scatter plots were examined for each. In these sixty-eight instances, the slopes were of this multiplicative sort, larger than 1.00, sixty-three times according to the net slope index.

In 1967, we presented the puzzle, explored a variety of considerations, and did extensive precautionary analyses, such as examining the effect for each trait separately and recomputing one matrix on ns of 25, 50, 100, and 200, in order to assure ourselves that it was a real puzzle. We noted that transforming our graphs by plotting r^2 or z' in place of r only exaggerated our puzzle and did not remove it. We wondered whether the basic model of factor analysis should be challenged not only for multitrait-multimethod matrices but for all uses, since we noted the abnormality of cumulative-additive relationships in explanatory theoretical mathematical models, as opposed to nonexplanatory predictive equations in the successful sciences, and we wondered whether factor analysis should be reformulated on a multiplicative basis. However, we did not suggest an adequate solution to our puzzle.

The Autoregressive Model

Because colleagues were also doing shotgun searches for causal relations in cross-lagged panel correlations, we had several multitrait-multitime matrices available. The most dramatic of these is shown in Figure 2E. As seen from our present perspective, this slope and its zero-zero intercept are exactly what would be expected from the most appropriate mathematical model available. In longitudinal or panel studies of intelligence, achievement, attitudes, and peer ratings involving several waves of measurement, it is regularly found that correlations are lower for longer time lapses than for intermediate lapses. This has come to be called the *simplex* pattern of correlations. This general pattern is compatible with an autoregressive model developed initially for long time series on a single individual or object. Usually, a first-order Markov process provides a good fit. In the simplest model, where one-occasion reliabilities in the main diagonal of the correlation matrix would be 1.00, a formula of this form is appropriate:

$$X_t = pX_{t-1} + x_t$$

where X is a score at time t or $t-1$, x_t is a new random component added in at time t and thereafter absorbed as a part of X, and p is a coefficient, less than 1.00, that can be interpreted as the correlation coefficient between X_t and X_{t-1} under stationary conditions.

It is usually inappropriate for the one-occasion reliabilities to be 1.00, so the preceding formula can be modified by interpreting the X as a latent score and generating the observed score X_t^* by this formula:

$$X_t^* = X_t + e_t$$

where e_t is a time-specific error that is not absorbed into the base for the next time period's X^* or X. That is, the autoregressive process is for the latent X rather than the observed X_t^*. In either case, correlations decrease over more time periods by a constant proportion p. Thus, if the syncronous $r_{X_t X_t} = .90$ and if $p = .80$, then

$$r_{X_t X_{t-1}} = .72, \ r_{X_t X_{t-2}} = .566, \ r_{X_t X_{t-3}} = .4528,$$

and so on, each correlation being .8 as large as the correlation for the next shorter time gap.

To extend this model to cross-trait, cross-time correlations, we need to assume that the latent factors explaining the intertrait correlations are autoregressive. The groundwork for an autoregressive mathematical model and analysis procedures for multitrait-multitime or -multioccasion matrices exist (Jöreskog, 1969, 1970; Jöreskog and Sörbum, 1980; Werts, Linn, and Jöreskog, 1977). These are both conceptually and empirically appropriate to the data of Figure 2E. They generate the expectation that a high synchronous correlation between two attitudes will be more attenuated or eroded over time than a low synchronous correlation. A synchronous correlation of zero can erode no further, and it remains zero when computed across a time lapse. The elegant intersection of the zero-zero origin of Figure 2E affirms the appropri-

102

Figure 2. Net Slopes for Similarity of Monomethod and
Heteromethod Estimates of Intertrait Correlations

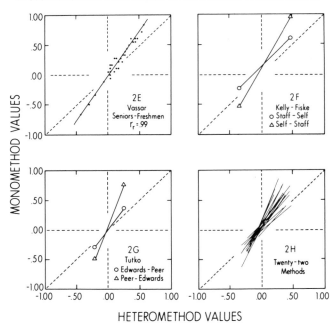

HETEROMETHOD VALUES

Note: In each case, the monomethod values are for the first method listed. (For 2E, substitute *time* for *method*. See text for explanation.)

ateness of such a model. (The r_r of .99 also implies that all the latent factors have the same p.) For multitime matrices, one could conceive of an augmentive additive or multiplicative spurious time-specific correlated error shared by all the measures taken on a specific occasion. But, for a data outcome such as form the Vassar freshman and senior retesting, a reductive imagery focused on the synchronous correlations, as truer than the time-spanning correlations, seems more appropriate than an augmentive imagery. Genuine changes in character and belief over the three-year period will undermine a high correlation more than they will a low one. Misidentification of responses from different persons on the two occasions as responses from the same person (this is perhaps unlikely in the Vassar study, but it is hard to completely avoid in a public opinion panel study) will disrupt a high correlation but not a zero correlation, and so forth.

Can this subtractive, erosion, dilution model be transferred from multitime matrices to multimethod matrices? As we noted in passing in 1967, the concept of attenuation of correlations as a result of the unreliability of measures has a multiplicative character, since high correlations are more attenuated by unreliability than low ones. The correction-for-attenuation algebra seems closer to the autoregressive model than to the additive model of factor analysis. Can we imagine attenuation as the result of invalidity as well as of unreliability? Can we conceive the values in the monomethod triangle as truer descriptions of the intertrait relationships, and the heteromethod triangles as an eroded, attenuated, corrupted version? (In the past, we must note, we have thought of the heteromethod values as purer, because they lacked the irrelevant augmentation produced by a method factor.)

Two types of considerations are relevant. The first is the fit of the data to the model, which we shall examine first. Even if we choose an augmentive methods-factor conceptualization in the end, the Jöreskog mathematical model could still be used to capture its multiplicative nature. However, the gestalt switch attempted here also requires the conceptualization of processes that make an attenuation or erosion model appropriate to multimethod matrices. We will attempt this on a case-by-case basis in the final section.

The Fit of the Autoregressive Model

To examine the data fit with the autoregressive model, we have performed a supplementary analysis of detailed tabular material presented in 1967 (Campbell and O'Connell, 1967). Here, as a result of the autoregressive model, we add an interest in the degree to which the net slope passes through the zero-zero intercept. Thus, the 1967 counterparts of Figures 1B, 1D, and 2E did not have the slopes drawn in, nor was the proximity with which that line passed through the zero-zero intercept commented upon. We have graphed the slope for eight validity studies, each involving two or three methods and one or two populations — a total of twenty-two methods. For these new graphs, only slopes, not scatters, are provided. Figure 2F is an example, showing the slopes for two methods (Staff and Self) examined by Kelly and Fiske (1951) when in the same matrix. (The lines are drawn for two σ's lengths above the means and for two below the means.) Self shows a slope of 1.02, with a constant elevation above the identity diagonal, and intercepts the vertical axis at .13, which corresponds to a mean elevation of .13, in perfect conformity with the additive method-factor model. When paired with Teammates (not presented here), Self shows a similar picture, with a slope of only 1.14, and intercepts the vertical axis at .12, approximating a mean elevation of .13. Table 2 presents all these values, together with background information on the number of traits, the number of persons being measured, and the intertrait pattern similarity index between monomethod and heteromethod triangles (r_r) (In Table 2 and in Figures F, G, and H, we depart from the 1967 article and Figures B, 1C, and D by pooling the two heterotrait-heteromethod triangles,

Table 2. Method Strength, Net Slope, and Intercepts
in Eight Validity Studies

	Background			Method Strength		Zero Intercepts	
	K	N	r_r	Elev.	Slope	Vert.	Hor.
Kelly-Fiske (1951)							
Staff/Teammates*	22	124	.75	.09	1.31	.05	– .04
Staff/*Teammates*	"	"	.82	.10	1.14	.08	– .07
Staff/Self	"	"	.54	.17	1.81	.12	– .07
Staff/*Self*	"	"	.48	.13	1.02	.13	– .13
Teammates/Self	"	"	.63	.17	1.77	.12	– .07
Teammates/*Self*	"	"	.46	.13	1.14	.12	– .11
Carroll (1952)							
Guilford-Martin/Peer	5	110	.57	.30	1.83	.18	– .10
Guilford-Martin/*Peer*	"	"	.80	.19	1.33	.14	– .11
Guilford-Martin/Self	"	"	.66	.17	1.68	– .01	.01
Guilford-Martin/*Self*	"	"	.54	– .07	.86	– .03	.04
Self/Peer	"	"	.14	.04	1.27	– .01	.00
Self/*Peer*	"	"	.64	.17	1.79	.05	– .03
Tutko							
Self/Peer	16	100	.68	.04	.91	.04	– .04
Self/*Peer*	"	"	.76	.08	2.06	.05	– .03
Self/Edwards	"	"	.45	.00	1.34	– .02	.01
Self/*Edwards*	"	"	.56	.02	1.30	.01	– .00
Peer/Edwards	"	"	.50	.16	2.68	.08	– .03
Peer/*Edwards*	"	"	.46	.01	1.42	– .01	.01
Meeland (Becker, 1960)							
Peer/Cattell AFHL	4	102	.62	.27	1.30	.17	– .13
Peer/*Cattell AFHL*	"	"	.50	– .05	1.15	– .10	.09
Wetzel (Peterson, 1965)							
Self/Parent	24	72	.54	.06	1.61	.01	– .01
Self/*Parent*	"	"	.43	.08	1.68	.03	– .02
Self/Peer	"	"	.56	.10	1.38	.09	– .07
Self/*Peer*	"	"	.60	.13	1.50	.12	– .08
Parent/Peer	"	"	.42	.14	1.65	.13	– .08
Parent/*Peer*	"	"	.55	.11	1.87	.09	– .05
Banta							
Fathers/Mothers	21	500	.68	.02	1.31	.00	– .00
Fathers/*Mothers*	"	"	.68	.04	1.30	.02	– .02
Projection Project							
Self/Peer (Fem)	27	204	.50	.21	2.29	.19	– .08
Self/*Peer* (Fem)	"	"	.55	.27	2.48	.24	– .10
Self/Peer (Male)	27	200	.60	.14	1.42	.13	– .09
Self/*Peer* (Male)	"	"	.68	.30	2.52	.23	– .09
Holtzman et al. (1963)							
Individual/Group	18	100	.75	.02	1.45	– .02	.01
Individual/*Group*	"	"	.76	.06	1.40	.02	– .02

*Italics indicate the method to which the row values apply.

rather than relating each separately to each monomethod triangle, thus reducing the number of indices to be considered by half.) The elevation column summarizes the strength of the method factor under the additive model, that is, the difference between the average intertrait correlation in the mono-method and heteromethod blocks. The slope is the net slope.

Also in the Kelly-Fiske data, one estimate for Teammate as a method (when paired with Staff) approaches the additive model, with a slope of 1.14, but the other estimate for Teammate (when paired with Self) has a slope of 1.77. In Table 2, there are only two other cases of slopes near 1.00 or below, and these occur in instances where the elevation measure indicates no method variance (Tutko Self, when paired with Peer, and Meeland Catell AFHL).

Figure 2G shows the Edwards Personal Preference Schedule (PPS), plus Taylor Manifest Anxiety as a sixteenth variable, and Peer ratings on the same variables from Tutko's unpublished study. (At Northwestern University around 1962, Thomas A. Tutko collected data from fraternities and other residential groups. In addition to taking the Edwards Schedule and the Taylor scale, subjects rated themselves and coresidents on scales intended to tap the sixteen test dimensions.) Here, the Edwards conforms to the autoregressive model by going through the zero-zero origin. In Table 2, the last two rows present the net slope's zero intercepts on the vertical axis and on the horizontal axis, in an effort to convey numerically the net slope's proximity to the zero-zero origin. For the Edwards of Figure 2G, these values are − .01 and .01; for the Vassar seniors and freshmen of Figure 2E, they are − .02 and .02. The other five multitrait-multitime matrices in our 1967 paper give intercept values generally close to zero, although some are as large as .03 and − .03, and this might be taken as a tentative upper limit for a purely autoregressive model.

Figure 2H plots net slopes for the twenty-two separate methods of Table 2. (Where there are three methods, Table 2 presents two slopes for each method. To reduce the redundancy that results, only the first that occurs has been plotted, although, as we have noted for the Teammates of Kelly and Fiske, the two are sometimes quite different.) If we take Figure 2H as an overall summary, we can draw a number of tentative conclusions. The multiplicative nature of method factors is preponderant. The narrowest pinch of the sheaf of slopes is nearer the zero-zero origin than to anything else, but it is also generally biased away from it in the upper left direction. The same fact is shown numerically in the column for vertical intercept in Table 2, where most of these values are positive, with only a third of them being equal to or less than the .03 maximum found in the multitime matrices, the median being .09. The horizontal intercepts are predominantly negative, that is, to the left of the origin, the median being − .05.

There is a slight bias in the same upper left direction for the multitime matrices, since nine tenths of the vertical intercepts are positive (median .02). It is possible that such bias is an artifact of the predominantly positive values ensured by our reflection of variables to that end and that it is made larger for the validity matrices by their lower r_r. However, it seems more likely that, for the validity matrices with large vertical intercepts, an additive method component is combined with a multiplicative process.

It is worth remarking, however, that a number of methods have substantial slopes that pass through the origin. To recapitulate, these include the Holtzman Ink Blot study, both individual and group methods, the Banta* study of 500 youths rated by both father and mother on twenty-one variables, and both the Edwards PPS and the Self ratings of Tutko's study. For these, at least, an attempt to conceptualize processes that would be more like attenuation than multiplicative augmentation seems worthwhile. (It is also conceivable that an augmentation model could employ the mathematics of the autoregressive or correction-for-attenuation form to improve on factor analysis for validity matrix summarization.)

Attenuation Versus Multiplicative Augmentation

Let us examine some specific examples and see what we can do to add realistic content to the attempted reconceptualization. We confess in advance that we are such long-standing participants in the old augmentation paradigm of halo effects, response sets, correlated error, and shared method-specific content-irrelevant variance that we may not give the new paradigm a fair shake.

Let us start with the study by Holtzman and others (1963). Individuals took both form A and form B, one in group administration (no examiner inquiry, recording their own responses on record forms, and so on), the other in the individual administration typical of the Rorschach test. Each form had a different set of blots, and although the sets were selected for equivalent average drawing power, each blot set stimulated somewhat different responses. Heterogeneity in small stimuli samples attenuates relationships that would be stronger if each form was infinitely long. A correction for test length is in order, in the attenuation mode. For relationships between variables within one form, the specific ink blots are, of course, the same, and the diluting effects of short test length are reduced. This is how an erosion attenuation model could read. But, note how easily this gestalt slips back into the augmentation mode. The sampling of both blots and responses involves chance sampling errors. Within a given form, correlation of two traits involves corre-

---

*In 1967 (Campbell and O'Connell, 1967), we called this the Banta study, because we obtained the data from Thomas J. Banta during his postdoctoral period at Northwestern University in 1959–60. The data came from Leonard Eron's Rip Van Winkle Foundation study. A partial report, based on an N of 50, appears in Eron and others (1961). Banta's matrix had been computed on a missing-data program that provided different Ns for each correlation, averaging around 500. Twenty-one behavior traits or rating variables were employed, and data were secured from both fathers and mothers.

lation of sampling error. When each trait is measured by a separate form, this correlated error is absent, and the correlations are, therefore, lower. To fit these data, the correlated error must augment high basic correlations, not zero correlations. If a given response to a given aspect of a blot is validly scored for both of two dimensions, then those two dimensions have some intrinsic correlation. Chancy, stochastic aspects in the emission of such a response will exaggerate such intrinsic correlation when it is correlated within the same administration of the same form. Nothing that we have come up with here would be unique to a validity study, in contrast to a multitrait two-administration reliability matrix. Holtzman and others (1963) offered such matrices for both group-group and individual-individual, but we did not analyze them in our paper of 1967.

In three of the studies, multiple structured-item self-description personality questionnaires are compared with peer ratings, self-ratings, or both. In Carroll's (1952) study of five factor scores from the Guilford-Martin inventory, some single-item responses were scored for more than one factor. This was done where the factors were intrinsically correlated, and the multiple scoring introduces correlated error that would amplify the correlations. Where two trait-scoring keys shared no items, no correlated error would be added, and the base correlation would be apt to be zero. (Carroll's study has only five traits, and hence it has only ten intertrait correlations on which to base r_n, net slope, and so forth; as a consequence, the results are quite unstable.)

The practice of using one item response on more than one trait's scoring key is lacking in the Edwards PPS study. In both of its pairings in Tutko's study, the Edwards fits the autoregressive model well, and our handiest correlated-error multiplicative enhancement model is not obviously appropriate. Can we come up with an attenuation, erosion, subtractive model? We will try: The single-sentence, nine-response level rating scales employed were devised in an attempt to epitomize the variables tapped by the questionnaire. This attempt was inevitably imperfect, and the imperfection attenuated high intertrait correlations more than it did low ones. The imperfect translation hypothesis is supported by one detail from our 1967 paper. When all the methods use the same rating scales (for example, Staff, Teammates, and Self in the study by Kelly and Fiske, 1951), the r_r between the two monomethods tends to be as high or higher than the r_r between one monomethod and the heteromethod triangle; for the Edwards study, this is not so. While Peer and Self monomethods produce an r_r of .72, they correlate with the Edwards monomethod only .18 and .19, very weakly indeed. That the monohet r_rs in the Edwards are as high as .45–.56 is remarkable indeed. For the Edwards PPS, the erosion, reductive model seems more plausible than the augmentive, correlated-error, add-on-of-irrelevant-methods variance model.

Seven of the eight studies involve personality ratings with a single rating scale per trait. For six studies, two or three of the other, separate methods employed for analysis involve separate classes of raters who use identical rating scales to describe the same persons. It is on these six studies that we will focus our final speculations. Let us first address an extreme that is not exemplified by any of the studies that we examine here: Two raters each rate 100 persons on twelve personality scales. The ratings are made independently, and they are based on independent samples of each person's behavior. The two raters do not share a common community of gossip about the personalities of those whom they rate. They do, however, agree on meanings for the personality trait terms. Each behavior sample can provide valid information on more than one personality trait. The small number and difference of the behavior samples attenuate the correlations across raters. Greatly increasing the number of samples that each rater has for comparable social settings will reduce this attenuation, even if the specific samples continue to have no overlap. Increasing the sample size will make their samples more nearly equivalent to having the same sample, thus, making the heterorater intertrait correlations more like the monorater correlations. For short and distinct behavior samples, the monorater correlations are more like those hypothetical asymptotic large-sample correlations. The heterorater correlations are attenuated versions of them, more attenuated for the high monorater values.

This is the best that we can do for a reductive, erosion model. It may have a certain amount of validity as part of the explanation for the higher correlations in the monomethod blocks. However, even in this idealized scenario, the case for an augmentation model may seem stronger. The small behavior samples have chance unrepresentativeness or sampling error. This is correlated error for trait ratings by the same rater, and it is probably more enhancing for high intertrait relations than for low ones. Large-sample asymptotic values will be different from small-sample values, and the correlations would probably be lower, if behavior sampling were the only problem involved.

Exemplified by higher correlations when third variables are correlated with teacher-rated intelligence than with measured intelligence, halo effects in ratings were the first methods factor to be noted in the psychometric tradition—around 1920 or earlier. It is possible that halo effects were represented in our multitrait-multimethod matrix thinking as additive factors, but if they were, it was thoughtlessly done. From the very beginning, the halo effect involved rater theories of intertrait relationships, in which holding the theory created or at least augmented the correlations among ratings. Some theories may have been totally fictional, such as the belief that popular pupils make fewer errors in calisthenic drills, as in the Zillig (1928) study featured in Klineberg's (1940) influential social psychology text. Such popularly accepted false theories, and their specific attributions to individuals, will account for heterorater agreements under at least two conditions: if both raters share in a gossip community about the ratees (this is ruled out in the preceding scenario), or if one of the traits (such as physical beauty or talkativeness) is reliably noted by independent raters. In either condition, a rater's chance unevenness in diagnostic judgments, coupled with the theory that carries the related trait along, will produce higher monorater than heterorater correlations, thereby generating the multiplicative halo effect pattern. Schweder and D'Andrade (1980), Nisbett and Ross (1980), and Ross and Lepper (1980) review the extensive modern rediscovery and elaboration of such findings. Even where the theorized intertrait relationships have some grain of truth, they are exaggerated when they are noted at all. These exaggerated beliefs about relationships dominate the monorater correlations. It is probably the higher real correlations that are the most apt to be noted and exaggerated, thus providing the multiplicative form of the halo-effect correlation enhancement for even our simple insulated-rater ideal model. This will be the case even if the subjective personality theories or meanings given to the trait terms are identical. Idiosyncrasies in these regards will further increase the contrast between monorater and heterorater estimates of intertrait correlation. (Perhaps these idiosyncrasy effects should be regarded as attenuating the heterorater correlations.)

None of our personality-rating studies conforms to this simple scenario, where each of two independent raters (the two methods) rates all the ratees. For Carroll, Tutko, Meeland, and our Projection Project, the Peer ratings were collected from coresidents in student housing, who rated each other in clusters ranging from five to twenty or so. (On the Wetzel study, a unique peer, usually a roommate, was obtained for each ratee.) The average rating (excluding self-ratings) that each ratee received was used as the Peer rating. The Ns of 100 to 204 have been made up of a number of such clusters, both raters and ratees differing from cluster to cluster. Shared personality trait theories as a source of error augment intertrait correlations under this condition, while idiosyncratic ones tend to get averaged out. Insofar as there are trends, the peer ratings tend to show the strongest methods factors by both elevation and net slope; they may also show more nonzero intercepts. The Teammates in the study by Kelly and Fiske (1951) also were collected in small clusters. Staff was constant across all ratees, although its members experienced the latter by teams and had access to teammate ratings before making their own.

In another rating model, each ratee is rated by a different rater. Banta's study of 500 youths rated by both father and mother is typical. This study is noteworthy for its conformity to the autoregressive model, since the slope passes right through the zero-zero origin. In general, by either elevation or slope, the method factors were low. The Self ratings in all studies are also of this nature, and in general they have lower methods factors than the Peer ratings of the same study. They conform unevenly to the multiplicative model, as illustrated by Figure 2F. Insofar as all raters share a common subjective theory of personality, this should enhance monomethod correlations. The case for the attenuation model is no better here than in the two-rater scenario.

Overview

This chapter has called attention to an overlooked puzzle posed by methods factors in the use of multitrait-multimethod matrices in the personality domain. The authors have presented an alternative interpretation, in which differences in method attenuate relationships that are more validly shown when method is held constant than in cross-method correlations. This interpretation has been contrasted with the concept that shared method augments intertrait correlations above their true values, which are more validly shown in their heteromethod form. For the attenuation model, the autoregressive statistics of time series analysis could be considered appropriate, and many of the data sets show superficial conformity to it. When conceptualizing specific processes, however, a multiplicative augmentation model seems most appropriate in most instances. In this model, correlated error and rater theories of personality exaggerate the correlation between the more highly correlated traits.

References

Becker, W. L. "The Matching of Behavior Rating and Questionnaire Personality Factors." *Psychological Bulletin,* 1960, *57,* 201–212.

Campbell, D. T. "Methodological Suggestions from a Comparative Psychology of Knowledge Processes." *Inquiry,* 1959, *2,* 152–182.

Campbell, D. T. "Conformity in Psychology's Theories of Acquired Behavioral Dispositions." In I. A. Berg and B. M. Bass (Eds.), *Conformity and Deviation.* New York: Harper, 1961.

Campbell, D. T. "Pattern Matching as an Essential in Distal Knowing." In K. R. Hammond (Ed.), *The Psychology of Egon Brunswik.* New York: Holt, Rinehart and Winston, 1966.

Campbell, D. T., and Fiske, D. W. "Convergent and Discriminant Validation by the Multitrait-Multimethod Matrix." *Psychological Bulletin,* 1959, *56,* 81–105.

Campbell, D. T., and O'Connell, E. J. "Methods Factors in Multitrait-Multimethod Matrices: Multiplicative Rather Than Additive?" *Multivariate Behavioral Research,* 1967, *2,* 409–426.

Campbell, D. T., Siegman, C. R., and Rees, M. B. "Direction-of-Wording Effects in the Relationships Between Scales." *Psychological Bulletin,* 1967, *68,* 293–303.

Carroll, J. B. "Ratings on Traits Measured by a Factored Personality Inventory." *Journal of Abnormal and Social Psychology,* 1952, *47,* 626–632.

Chapman, L. J., and Campbell, D. T. "Response Set in the F Scale." *Journal of Abnormal and Social Psychology,* 1957, *54,* 129–132.

Eron, L. D., Banta, T. J., Walder, L. O., and Lovlicht, J. H. "Comparison of Data Obtained from Mothers and Fathers on Childrearing Practices and Their Relation to Child Aggression." *Child Development,* 1961, *32,* 457–472.

Holtzman, W. H., Mosely, E. C., Reinehr, R. C., and Abbott, E. "Comparison of the Group Method and the Standard Individual Version of the Holtzman Inkblot Test." *Journal of Clinical Psychology,* 1963, *19,* 441–449.

Jöreskog, K. G. *Factoring the Multitest-Multioccasion Correlation Matrix.* Research Bulletin 69-62. Princeton, N.J.: Educational Testing Service, 1969.

Jöreskog, K. G. "Estimation and Testing of Simplex Models." *The British Journal of Mathematical and Statistical Psychology,* 1970, *23,* 121–145.

Jöreskog, K. G., and Sörbom, D. *Advances in Factor Analysis and Structural Equation Models.* Cambridge, Mass.: Abt, 1979.

Kelly, E. L., and Fiske, D. W. *The Prediction of Performance in Clinical Psychology.* Ann Arbor: University of Michigan Press, 1951.

Klineberg, O. *Social Psychology.* New York: Henry Holt, 1940.

Nisbett, R. E., and Ross, L. *Human Inference: Strategies and Shortcomings of Social Judgment.* Englewood Cliffs, N.J.: Prentice-Hall, 1980.

Peterson, D. R. "Scope and Generality of Verbally-Defined Personality Factors." *Psychological Review,* 1965, *72,* 48–59.

Ross, L., and Lepper, M. R. "The Perseverance of Beliefs: Empirical and Normative Considerations." In R. A. Shweder (Ed.), *New Directions for Methodology of Social and Behavioral Science: Fallible Judgment in Behavioral Research,* no. 4. San Francisco: Jossey-Bass, 1980.

Shweder, R. A., and D'Andrade, R. G. "The Systematic Distortion Hypothesis." In R. A. Shweder (Ed.), *New Directions for Methodology of Social and Behavioral Science: Fallible Judgment in Behavioral Research,* no. 4. San Francisco: Jossey-Bass, 1980.

Werts, C. E., Linn, R. L., and Jöreskog, K. G. "A Simplex Model for Analyzing Academic Growth." *Educational and Psychological Measurement,* 1977, *37,* 745–756.

Yates, A. T. "Distinguishing Trait from Method Variance in Fitting the Invariant Common-Factor Model to Observed Intercorrelations Among Personality Rating Scales." Unpublished manuscript, 1980.

Zillig, M. "Einstellung und Aussage." *Zeitschrift für Psychologie,* 1928, *106,* 58–106.

Donald T. Campbell is New York State Board of Regents Albert Schweitzer Professor in the Maxwell School of Citizenship and Public Affairs at Syracuse University.

Edward J. O'Connell is professor of psychology in the Department of Psychology at Syracuse University.

Index

A

Abbott, E., 110

Ashmore, R. D., 41n

Assignment rule: and conclusion validity, 34–35; and construct validity, 35–36; incorrect definition of, 38; and independent variables, 34; and internal validity, 33–34; and number of conditions, 28–29, 32; and number of units, 32; random or nonrandom, and internal validities, 15; as research design distinction, 28–32; and units nested or crossed within conditions, 29–31; types of, 29

Autoregression model: analysis of, 100–103; fit of, 103–106

B

Ball, S., 31, 39

Banta, T. J., 104, 106, 109, 110

Becker, H. S., 41n, 42, 56

Becker, W. L., 104, 110

Bellettirie, G., 48, 57

Binomian effect-size display (BESD), 72–74

Birnbaum, M. H., 17, 20

Blumer, H., 55, 56

Bogatz, G. A., 31, 39

Borus, M. E., 31, 39

Bourne, E., 85, 91

Brewer, M. B., 17, 20

Brickman, P., 45, 56

Brinberg, D., 1–3, 5–21, 81

Bush, R. R., 67, 75

Buss, D. M., 78, 91

C

Cambridge-Somerville experiment, and face validity, 49–50

Campbell, D. T., 2, 14, 15, 16, 17, 20, 24, 28, 29, 31, 39, 77, 79, 80, 81, 84, 87, 90, 91, 93–111

Cantril, H., 54, 56

Carlsmith, T. M., 44, 56

Carroll, J. B., 104, 107, 109

Causes: and face validity, 42–47; and researchers and subjects as observers and actors, 42–45; theories and ideologies related to, 45–47

Chapman, L. J., 97, 110

Clark, C. X., 46, 56

Cochran, W. G., 68, 70, 72, 75

Cognitive dissonance research, and face validity, 44

Cohen, J., 61, 62, 65, 74

Cohn, E. S., 44, 45, 46, 48, 57

Collins, W. J., 84, 85, 92

Comparison validity: concept of, 14–15; in research process, 13

Conceptual domain: described, 6; and methodological domain, 7; prestudy activities in, 9–10; and substantive domain, 7; and value, 12, 19

Conclusion validity: and assignment rule, 34–35; defined, 24, 25; and incorrect definition of units, 37–38; and number of conditions, 34; and number of replications, 35; research design related to, 34–35; and units nested or crossed in conditions, 34

Conditions: concept of, 25; number of, and assignment rule, 28–29, 32; number of, and conclusion validity, 34; number of, and internal validity, 32–33; number of, in research designs, 25; units nested or crossed in, and assignment rule, 29–31; units within, and conclusion validity, 34; units within, and construct validity, 36; units within, and internal validity, 33; units within, in research design, 25–26

Connecticut, speed crackdown in, 28, 32

Construct validity: and assignment rule, 35–36; concept of, 15, 24, 25; and construct operationalization, 81; and face validity, 51–52; and generalizations, 24; and number of replications, 36; and number of units, 36; re-